PRAISE

For roughly 25 years, neuroscientists and theologians have been working together to explore and to ascertain whether the brain is the instigator or receiver of how individuals express deep feelings and experience religious beliefs. In this wonderful book, Sarah Flick brings together a lifetime of insights that changed her perspectives and practices as a clinical psychiatrist and compassionate spiritual director. *Desire, Mystery, and Belonging* illuminates heartfelt reflections that invite us to energize mind and soul. Dr. Flick invites all of us to contemplate what really matters, what ultimately embodies and distinguishes us as human beings on life's journey.

   – **W. Andrew Achenbaum**, Professor Emeritus,
   Consortium on Aging, Texas Medical Center

Sarah's storytelling is a tender, immersive expression of deeply soulful reflections. The invitation is right in front of us; *Desire, Mystery, and Belonging* leads us into fully realized experiences of presence and honoring. Sarah is a skilled observer and life traveler, and she lights the way here with a generous and compelling narrative through her life that leads us home to our own sense of self. Done with love, compassion, and an invitation to trust in our own deep knowing, *Desire, Mystery, and Belonging* is a treasure of a book!

   – **Sonya Joy**, Writer, Photographer, www.wildluminary.com

With profound clarity and warmth, Sarah Flick welcomes us into a nourishing exploration of the intersections of desire, mystery, and belonging in our own lives. I relished the storytelling in this book, feeling simultaneously entertained and deeply encouraged to understand my own path in this new, glorious light. Reading it felt like spending time with a friend discussing the mysteries of life in a way that was both really approachable and also soul nourishing. I found myself laughing and crying along with the words and nodding my head as I recounted the stories as I was navigating the rest of my daily life. This book is a must read for anyone hungry to live in greater alignment with their spirit and deep yearnings.

– **Mara Glatzel**, author of upcoming
Needy: The Path from Self-Abandonment to Self-Partnership
(Sounds True, 2023), www.maraglatzel.com

DESIRE

MYSTERY

and

BELONGING

A Spiritual Memoir

Sarah Robinson Flick, MD

INSPIREBYTES
OMNI MEDIA

Distributed globally with Expanded Distribution by KDP.

ISBN Paperback: 978-1-953445-21-6
ISBN E-Book: 978-1-953445-22-3
Library of Congress Control Number: 2021953426

▧ INSPIREBYTES OMNI MEDIA

Inspirebytes Omni Media LLC
PO Box 988
Wilmette, IL 60091

For more information, please visit www.inspirebytes.com.

To Bob and Katie, our family is the
great love and deep joy of my life.
I will always be so grateful for you.
I will love you forever and ever.

CONTENTS

Desire, Mystery, and Belonging

FOREWORD

by Jennifer Louden

What a marvelous treasure you hold in your hands, an intimate guide to desire, mystery, and belonging, three qualities we all need to live a life of meaning, beauty, and presence.

Maybe you haven't thought about desire, mystery, and belonging before now, how they relate to each other, how they become more together, or even named them as something you wanted to explore? That's part of what makes this book so special. Through the lens of her well-lived life, Sarah offers a startling fresh way of naming and relating to this powerful trio, and once you read her stories and thoughts, I hope what happened to me happens to you: you see the world and your possibilities anew.

I've had the honor of knowing Sarah, first as a student, then as a friend, for close to twenty years. I've been lucky to help her shepherd this book into your hands, to help her trust her stories and insights, and to watch her 'own' her desire to convey them from her depths as an offering of belonging.

Sarah is one of the most generous and trustworthy people I know, and this book is built from, and infused with, her lifelong exploration of the inner life, the communal life, of mental illness and mental health, of the religious life, and the call to create and be heard. You can trust her as your guide. Every word in this book has been placed there with great care.

What can you hope to learn from Sarah? Or why read this book? Don't you find the best books defy tidy summaries and instead change how you see yourself and the world? This book does that, through

Desire, Mystery, and Belonging

story, through vulnerability, by embracing desire, and by doing so, it takes you into the mystery of this moment, and to knowing, with your whole being, you belong and always have.

May your heart be nourished by Sarah's stories and insights, and in turn, may that nourishment stream into your world and nourish others.

Jen Louden
Longmont, Colorado
2021

A Prayer for This Book

Most Holy One,

Thank you for the time and space I have been given to write. Thank you for Taos, Garrison, Phoenicia, Pittsfield, Sedona, Litchfield, and Galveston. Thank you for all my family and teachers and friends who believed in my writing. Thank you for the resources that were mine to help me find the writing path.

I ask now that you bless this book. I ask that you give it the life that it is meant to have. I ask that I be relieved of anxiety about outcomes, and that I may trust in the journey going forward. Help me be willing to share. Help this book to land where it needs to land, where life wants it to land, where you long for it to land.

Please give me the courage and humility to take my own hands off the steering wheel. May I sit in the driver's seat while trusting the road to be just as it is. Allow me to open my mind and heart and spirit to what comes next and to not be afraid of uncertainty. Let me be an earthen vessel for the messages of desire, mystery, and belonging.

Help me to trust. I pray for wholeness and for a loving heart. May I and those I love and those who will read these words always know that all is well, and all will be well.

In the name of the one who walked on water in the beautiful blue Sea of Galilee,

Amen.

A Letter to the Reader

Dear Reader,

I am writing to you to share why I have written this story.

I don't think that life can be tidy. We might live in houses that are clean, and we might have an orderly calendar. Our closets may be organized, and every room may have fresh flowers. Maybe we are lucky enough to have everything happen right on time. Maybe we are lucky enough to have everything we really need.

But even if this movie set of a life were all perfectly in place around you, it would still be external. None of this guarantees that it will take root inside you. Our outsides can be gorgeous while our insides are howling in chaos. I don't think anybody is tidy on the inside. As a psychiatrist and spiritual director, I have been honored to sit with and listen to people from all walks of life in many different settings. Some of them have had enormous struggles in life. Some have known great blessings. But all of their insides were dark forests and underground caves and dry deserts where doubt and pain and anxiety and anger wandered freely alongside joy and excitement and tenderness and hope. Their insides were just like mine, and they were not tidy. Not by a long shot.

I was never "the expert." I never will be. I have traveled a spiritual path with twists and turns and surprising, steep cliffs, just like all humans do.

There are so many ways to approach the Holy. So many traditions, so many rituals, so many stories.

Desire, Mystery, and Belonging

I am writing this story about just one more way to consider the journey. I have learned that we move in and out of seasons during our lives. We just want a simple map, a GPS, an Uber driver to navigate for us.

But the map and the GPS and the Uber driver are all outside of us. They can fit into their places in our tidy outsides. But our insides—our wild, vulnerable, tender insides—need a different kind of guidance, because life is not a linear journey.

This story is about a life. About a family. About friends and the world we all inhabit. It is not tidy, and there is no real ending. Not yet.

More than anything else, here's what I really want you to know: There are many ways to journey to wholeness, to walk into the Holy. I have come to know and believe that my deepest desire is not for a new car, or a new purse, or a summer vacation—my deepest desire is for a trustworthy guide through life. I desire peace. I desire healing. I desire love in all its faces. I am telling this story to honor desire, her sidekick companion, mystery, and the trustworthy bridge between them, belonging. I have come to know that they travel together like sisters.

Desire, mystery, and belonging get bad raps these days. Real, true, deep desire and unknowable, uncertain, unfathomable mystery are not convenient. We have a lot of information available in our world, so we don't need to stay in the dark. Or so we are told all day and all night, every day and every night. Even belonging can be seen as weak in our climate of anxiety and self-serving narcissism.

This story is an invitation to you. To make friends with desire, and with mystery, and with belonging. To trust that you can't do it wrong. To walk holding space for desire, mystery, and belonging in your heart, and to know the grace they can bring.

May desire beckon and welcome you as you explore. May mystery remind you of what we cannot know as you hunger for truth. May belonging light and warm your path. May you come to be where you need to be, and may you come home in the land of grace and wholeness.

Wishing you so many blessings on your way,
Sarah

In the Beginning:
An Invitation

"If you want to know God, follow your deepest desire." My beloved husband, an Episcopal priest, has paraphrased the Franciscan St. Bonaventure's quotation with these words as long as I have known him. I have heard him say these words while preaching and while in conversation for over thirty years now. When I first heard him say this, I was finishing medical school, and I wondered what these words meant. I heard him say to others, "Be the most you that you can be... that is God's deepest desire for you, and that is the way that you will know your own deepest desire that God has planted in your heart." Or something like that. As a newly minted psychiatrist, I was caught up in these words. Had I not followed my deepest desire by going to medical school? Or had I? And how exactly do you know your deepest desire?

Our spiritual journey through life is often shaped by what we know or don't know of the Holy, of the ineffable, of all that we hold sacred in our lives. Bonaventure named this "God." I have known this Holy as God in my life, and in this book, I will use the name God for what I believe to be the Holy. Please know as you read this that there are many names for the Holy, and while my journey has been through various flavors of the Christian tradition, I believe as we approach the Holy, whatever name you may call it, through whatever tradition we understand (including no tradition), our common humanity allows us to share much of the journey.

Over my years as a psychiatrist and later as a spiritual director and later still as a writer, I have come to believe that as our world grows more complex, the meaning of desire, much less our deepest desires, scattered and hid. I want to know the Holy, and I have come to trust, like Bonaventure and my husband, that reaching for our deepest desires is how we know God. But the way is not clear and is filled with mystery. Belonging has been the key for me to unlocking this path and traveling in community.

I have come to believe that desire and mystery walk hand in hand throughout our spiritual journey. We seek our true desire by journeying through mystery, supported by belonging. We cannot know desire unless we consent to mystery. And, in a world overwhelmed by information from all directions, I believe that it is our deepest desire that can accompany us through mystery, through the unknowable, even through the unimaginable. Mystery is inevitable, and desire is a trustworthy compass. I have come to believe this in relationship with others, in relationship with myself, in relationship with the Holy. It is through belonging, through connection, through community that courage and strength arise and grow within us, around us, and beyond us. It is here that we find both wholeness and the Holy.

In this book, I explore desire and mystery and belonging and their relationship to a spiritual path. I share stories from my own life and spiritual journey, so this book is part memoir. I also write as a psychiatrist and a spiritual director exploring the twists and turns that arise as we human beings journey, including how we might experience and navigate challenging times.

My hope is that this book will offer an opportunity to reflect and spend time with yourself, your life, and your spiritual journey. My stories are only about me, but they may remind you of yourself. We share much of the same human experience. I wanted to create a space where reading and reflecting could be an invitation to desire, mystery, and belonging in the context of the Holy. For me, reflection is apparent grace. It has become a path to wholeness for me, though my journey is far from complete. There are far more questions than answers, but it is only time and space that separate us. And it is in this, our internal time and space, that we come to know the power and the grace of desire, of mystery, and of belonging.

May we braid what we know and what we don't know together. May we reach out for and lean into wholeness. May we travel together like bright ribbons streaming across the planet, moving always toward home.

Where I Come From

I am a child of the South. All the good and all the bad. Well, maybe just some of the bad. I was born into the frost of autumn, the reprieve from heat that finally arrives right before Thanksgiving. I was born into cornbread dressing and fried okra and two kinds of fruitcake.

I was born into Christmases overflowing with tradition and handmade stockings on the mantel. I was born into store window displays and parades. I was not born into snowy winters, but still I was born into wool coats and hats and mittens with strings.

I was born into Easter dresses and white gloves and straw bonnets with little silk flowers. I was born into dogwood and azaleas and pink and soft baby blues.

I was born into beloved summers. I was born into lazy beaches and lightning bug evenings. I was born into "Mother May I" and "1 2 3 Red Light." I was born into iced tea and rocking chairs on the porch.

I was born into heat. I was born in Southern Georgia, near pecan groves and plantations. I was born into roses.

The South is a feast for the senses. It is filled with lushness and dark nights and water, filled with lakes and oceans and rivers and ponds and creeks. The smell of honeysuckle speaks to God's creation all by itself. The South is feeling sweat trickling down your neck and tasting fried chicken and hearing church bells. It is these imprints, in my experience, that remain in my soul like traces of the ancestors before me.

I was born into the South.

All the good and some of the bad.

I was born into graciousness and I was born into rules. I was born into family honor and family faith.

I was born into a family that was Presbyterian on one side and Methodist on the other side. My maternal grandfather was a circuit rider Methodist minister.

I was born into a family that honored rules and also broke them, broke them when it was a calling of faith or irresistible delight.

The soil, the red Georgia clay, that was tilled and made ready for my arrival was fertilized with values of family and of faith.

I was the first grandchild on one side of the family and the second on the other side. I was baptized as an infant by my Methodist minister grandfather. My mother was a preacher's kid in a time where ministers moved every three years. She and my father met in the sixth grade, and neither ever looked at or loved another.

I was cradled in the stew of all of these ingredients. There was never a time when I was not surrounded by believers. And so the call to enter life open to God's invitation must have been irresistible to my soul, and though my delivery was long and complicated and required forceps to pull me out of my mother, I was born ready for life.

My beginnings were Methodist in flavor, and even my early baptism allowed me to claim the faith of my grandfather, who said yes to God's call. I was literally born into faith from my mother's womb.

As a child, my family belonged to the Presbyterian church. Because of their hospitality for children, I remember feeling welcome throughout those days, in Sunday school, in "joining the church," in choir, and in summer camp. The experience of being welcomed was for me a sign that the mysteries of life were best approached in community, and that beyond belonging lay love and happiness.

The Beginnings of the Interplay Between Desire, Mystery, and Belonging in My Life

As an older adolescent and young adult, the dynamic of conversion enveloped me. Driven by (a seemingly unnamed) desire, I explored

Roman Catholicism throughout college and learned of discernment as I practiced saying yes: Yes to becoming Catholic; Yes to two years of service as a Jesuit volunteer; Yes to a vocation to medicine, including four years of medical school and five years of residency training in adult and child psychiatry; and finally, Yes to marriage and motherhood. It was the season of being called and answering. Called into mystery, into belonging, and again into desire. It was a journey of friendship becoming love and love becoming family.

Once "grown up" and practicing medicine as a married mother, my faith journey was challenged by many demands and not enough community. It was paradoxically a time of much productivity, both personally and professionally, but very little spiritual sustenance. It was a time of being "Catholic" without participating in Catholic life. I learned about the longing my internal spirit held for external support and affirmation.

Enter the Episcopal church just down the street.

Episcopalianism is a denomination that is both Catholic and Protestant, liturgical and evangelical, with room for questions, concern for justice, and love for community. It felt like home. In short order, my husband and I were received into this church and our daughter was baptized. Soon thereafter, my husband re-entered active ministry (more on that later) as he was received into the Episcopal priesthood.

This season was a time of being seen, of being acknowledged, of supporting ministry in new ways. It was a time of great obligation as well as a time of great encouragement. The Episcopal church, with sprinklings of Quaker experience, offered what I needed at the time to navigate middle adulthood and to create and serve, again consenting to mystery in the context of belonging and finding myself in the house of desire.

Through all of these experiences, I have known grace. There have been seasons of struggle and moments of awe. I am beginning to know that my own spiritual journey spirals again and again from mystery, through belonging, and into desire, and that it is this journey that makes meaning for me. It is this rhythm that makes me whole. It is this pattern that seems to be the chorus of my hymn—my hymn of lament and my hymn of praise.

I write now to explore this rhythm in the contexts of seasons of experience, seasons of the life cycle, and seasons of diverse affiliations. This book is a love letter to desire, mystery, and belonging. I have seen this pattern, and it has held me, challenged me, and healed me. I have practiced medicine now for thirty years, and I am absolutely sure of the connections between mind, body, and spirit. We are never actually fully healed, and we are never actually fully lost. We live in the middle, and we are always becoming. Yet, no matter where we are in this cycle, we are always surrounded by grace.

Now, walking into the threshold of retirement, my heart wonders what season comes next. What I will be invited into, I do not yet know. I do believe that it will again require entering into mystery. I pray that the blessing of belonging will continue to brighten the journey. I hope that beyond the invitation lies the final desire, the love of the Holy One and the wholeness of the Spirit.

DESIRE, MYSTERY, BELONGING

Chapter 1

DESIRE, MYSTERY, BELONGING

The most direct way for me to explore the interplay between desire, mystery, and belonging is to tell stories and follow how they show up alone, lead into each other, and join forces to support us. I chose seven areas of life to reflect on:

- love
- work
- family
- grace
- creativity
- healing and wholeness
- death and letting go

For each of these areas I share personal stories and reflections of my own. As a way of introduction, I'd like to start with a brief overview of what this trio can offer in the forthcoming pages.

Desire shares the story of a beautiful day in Italy. This story is about our senses, how what we see, hear, taste, touch, and smell can unlock the door to desire. It is a story about how the beauty around us—in nature or created—can reflect our desire.

As we discover our inner desire mirrored in the world around us, we learn to celebrate our desire as well as the beauty. Our desire invites us more deeply into the longings of our heart, of who we truly are in our innermost being.

Mystery tells a story about questions that arise spontaneously in conversations with a stranger. There are moments when we might feel unsteady and unsure of what to say or do in an unfamiliar context.

More often than not, our experience of mystery is an invitation to stay still, to ponder, to wonder about choices we have made and will make. We meet a stranger, and a new world of reflection opens. Our experience of mystery teaches us to wait, to be patient, to find peace in the stillness of now.

Belonging offers a story that holds a rainbow of experiences of connection that are about belonging to ourselves, to others, to our world, and to the Holy. Some belonging we inherit from others, and some we choose for ourselves. All of it matters.

Belonging is the scaffolding that honors our desire and supports us when we encounter times of mystery, of the unknown, of uncertainty. Whether lifelong or momentary, our experience of belonging teaches us to trust, to hope, and to find comfort and stability in the ebbs and flows of life itself.

The thing about telling stories is that we all remember our own experience. All the stories in this book are told as I remember them. Families, friends, colleagues, and others will remember them differently. The invitation here is to offer stories as starting points, as beginnings for my exploration and for yours, the reader's, of desire, mystery, and belonging on your own spiritual journey. May these stories remind you of your own spirit, of your own stories, and of the wholeness that beckons in your own life.

Chapter 2

DESIRE

A Sunday afternoon in Montebudello. The cool breeze flows softly and lightly across my forehead as I turn to start down the hill. I look out across acres and acres of the green that is only seen in spring. The "Easter basket green" comes in all different shapes: grass waving, grapevines, trees with budding leaves, moss at the edge of ponds. This tender green of new life, of fragile hope, of vulnerable beginnings. There are no clouds in the bright blue sky to obscure the golden sun beaming warmth down on us.

This is what desire feels like to me today.

The tangy bite of hard Parmesan cheese on my tongue. The bubbles of Prosecco tickling my cheeks. The pickled peppers giving my mouth twinges of sourness. The warm bread in my hands. The homemade penne pasta that's so easy to chew. The aromatic ragu falling in my tummy and warming my whole body. The cherry tomatoes. The grape and apple pie. The light Lambrusco. The enormous strawberries dipped in chocolate.

This is what desire tastes like to me today.

Writing about desire raises many questions. What is desire, and why does it matter? Desire wears many faces and walks many paths. Like St. Bonaventure, an early follower of St. Francis of Assisi in the 1200s, I have come to believe that following our deepest desire is how we know God. Desire is a feeling, a knowing, a longing. This desire is to be all of ourselves, to be the most ourselves that we can be. This desire is not the desire of the world. It is not the desire we are offered by the media, social or otherwise. It is not on Facebook or Instagram or Snapchat or in a magazine or on a TV show.

This desire does not come from outside of us. This desire is not imposed on us or growing in someone else's mind to manipulate us. This desire is rooted in the part of us that lies deep within, the place where we are open to what we don't know, the place where we become who we are and where we tend the eternal flame of our very being.

This desire—this deepest desire—is the way home. The way home to our center, the way home to our soul. We reach the Holy not through what others tell us to think or believe or value, but rather through our honest openness to becoming who we are, who we know ourselves to be when no one else is around. This is a lifelong journey. Some believe we are born already knowing this connection and that we lose it almost immediately as we learn to conform to the world around us.

And yet days in the gracious presence of an Italian countryside—like the ones I am living as I write this chapter—can hold up a mirror for us. We can listen to our bodies as they receive the goodness of the sun, the light in a loved one's eyes, or the breeze's caress, and we can know thankfulness. We can listen to our bodies and invite our minds and our souls to join in. I believe that desire calls all parts of us into wholeness. But we only experience this when we can touch the connection between wholeness and holiness, when we can allow ourselves to look at ourselves and know the beloved there.

My own desires have changed over the years. I have often desired safety—safety from that which I did not want, did not desire. It took me a long time to see deeper into the flame of desire that transcends safety, to know that there is a constant light deep within that is the path to freedom. That what comes from that place is my "deepest desire" and is who I really am. That place of desire is the Holy. It gathers all the parts of beauty, grace, and peace that I see outside of myself and all the pieces of mercy, reverence, and love that I experience inside myself and braids them all together into an eternal flame. My fears have begun to soften in this light. I have very slowly begun to hear and trust the guidance of this desire in my life over the years.

As a child, I spent whole days in the library in the summers reading the likes of Louisa May Alcott, Madeleine L'Engle, and A.A. Milne. Books were a constant companion as I have always needed quiet time to fill my well in order to be in the world and serve as best I could. Sometimes I want to laugh realizing now how the God who created and loves me was inside me all along. I knew and trusted the Jesus who lived in my heart. I was not as clear about knowing and trusting my heart itself.

In truth, the world outside me has invited me to learn from the world inside me. This takes time and patience and trust. It also takes courage. And intention. And traveling lightly with an open mind and a willing heart.

None of this came naturally to me. As an oldest child and a physician, I lived on responsibility for many years. I come from a family that served others and valued goodness, and I knew this legacy from a very early age. I honor those years, and I love remembering the moments of learning, discovery, and growing. I have known deep connections through the journey of becoming a healer and a writer.

For me, this journey into the deepest desire has required the acceptance of mystery, the acknowledgment that we cannot know everything that we might want or need to know. We cannot foretell the future, or even what might happen later today. Yet we live in this culture of immediate gratification where everyone carries phones that we can use to access almost anything at any moment. Almost as soon as a question occurs to me, I find myself searching online for the answer. I want to know right away. Yet all the smartphone answers are the answers outside of me, and therefore they are limited.

The answers to questions of true discernment come from that deep place within me.

What work should I do?

Who should I love?

How do I become free?

What am I called to?

How can I be wholly who I am?

I think these are the questions to which we can't find answers from our phones. And for me, these are the questions that make all the difference.

Encountering our deepest desire almost always means that we need to learn to tolerate and live with mystery, to accept that we do not and cannot know everything. We can learn to live as life itself unfolds—with patience and grace and trust.

How do we travel this path?

It seems counterintuitive, but for me, these inquiries that we make by ourselves have been most fruitful in the company of others. I have been able to learn to tolerate mystery, or, as some say, tolerate ambiguity, through the practice of belonging.

Community matters to me. My faith rests on both my relationship to the Holy and my relationship to my brothers and sisters, known to me and unknown to me. I believe that my deepest desire will lead me to the presence of the Holy, but only if I can allow for mystery, and only if I practice belonging in community. I am not made for myself alone. I have a connection to those I know and love and a connection to those I will never meet but who are as human as I am.

And so this is how I see desire. The deepest desire is reflected in the world around me and kindled somewhere deep inside me. The union of body and mind and spirit. The beginning again. The Holy and the whole. The questions that we begin asking and may never answer. The journey alongside each other.

The cycle that has marked my own journey, and the journeys of those who I have seen in spiritual direction, is that as we search for our deepest desire, we will encounter mystery: the unknown and sometimes the unknowable. Mystery can be unexpected and joyous as well as painful. To follow desire, we must consent to mystery. The mystery, if we are faithful, will lead us again to desire. For me, the bridge between the two has been belonging—a sense of community and relationship with others. And so I see this desire—this wholeness in holiness—braided repeatedly with mystery and supported by belonging.

This cycle of desire and mystery and belonging has been my spiritual path. It has led me over and over again to discovery of wholeness, of surprise, of knowing home. It has led me to grace.

There is a new rose blooming today here on our patio in Bologna. This private courtyard is a magic place. We walk down a spiral staircase of black iron to get there. No one can come in but us. All last week, the flowering plants had buds. Signs of hope. There is an olive tree, a rose bush, a bed of rosemary, pots of jasmine and camellias, and ivy on the brick walls. And today, one glorious rose is blooming in the sunlight. It is supposed to rain today. I am not much of a gardener at home, but here in Italy, this one new rose sings to me of desire. It wasn't here yesterday and may not last long in the rain to come. Our hosts have planted these beautiful living seeds, trusting in the blooms to come. And we are here to see and to know that this desire contains everything we ever need. The secret of life itself resides in this lovely, brightly-colored single rose.

May we have the willingness to see the loveliness of life all around us and to allow this beauty to kindle the flame of desire deep within us. May we know the bravery of living in mystery, of accepting our humanity, of practicing patience and waiting for what we do not yet know. May we honor each other and reach out when we feel called to do so, seeking and offering compassion and light and grace. And in this, may we know the Holy, and may we know wholeness around us, within us, and beyond us.

Chapter 3

MYSTERY

I am sitting in my stateroom on a river cruise ship, looking out at the vineyards and forests of Germany. The sky is bright blue. Every now and then, we glide past campgrounds filled with tents and campers, local residents on summer holiday. Sometimes we slowly pass through tiny villages, some of which look like fairy tales that have come to life.

As we gaze out at the scenery (so luscious that I can almost taste it!) my mind wanders back home. Home to Texas, where I spent the last few days before our departure frantically trying to organize information about the small children and babies we had just learned were coming to a makeshift shelter in Houston after they had been separated from their parents at the border. As I fielded calls and emails, I should have been packing for this trip. Truthfully, I should have packed some days before, but with three days to go before we left, I thought I would be able to pack at a leisurely pace, the way I like to.

Instead, I woke up early on a Saturday morning to the news of the little ones coming to Houston, and I was hijacked until almost the moment we boarded the plane. I couldn't stop reading, emailing, thinking, and gathering friends online to explore courses of action. What could we do to help? I hadn't felt this much passion for a social justice issue in a long time. Becoming increasingly overwhelmed and numbed by the daily barrage of news—both true and false—related to President Trump, I was lucky that I remembered to squeeze in toothpaste and underwear for the trip!

Desire, Mystery, and Belonging

Yesterday, after we docked in Heidelberg and toured a giant castle complex, we had lunch with local university students. I sat next to a young man who had grown up nearby and was completing a graduate degree in economics. As we chatted, the subject of President Trump arose in the conversation.

The student was quick to assure us that although he and his friends worried about who would now "lead the free world," they knew and understood that this president did not speak for all Americans. As a student of economics, he expressed concern for the world economy in the context of trade changes made in the name of the United States. But he was clear that he would not "blame" our whole country for this fallout. He acknowledged that while previous presidents have been seen as representatives of the country, the current president was not seen as fully representative of the United States. I shared with him my fear for the little ones separated from their loved ones, and he nodded in understanding.

As our conversation went on, we talked about religion. Once my husband Bob identified himself as an Episcopal priest, our lunch companion said that he was an atheist. He shared that he was baptized Christian but came to question the existence of God as he grew older. He said, "You can either do good works to make God happy, or because doing good works is the right thing to do. The outcome is the same. I choose to do good works for the rightness of doing them." My husband replied with, "I find that I am able to be more faithful to helping others with the support of belonging to a community."

Bob went on to say, "For me, faith is more about relationships than doing good works." The student listened closely, as I sat at the table and realized that this was another moment of the cycle of desire, mystery, and belonging. The desire to believe (in something, in anything?), the mystery of the unknown and the unknowable, and the support of belonging to a community, all moving together to give birth to a moment of spirit, a moment of grace. As we said goodbye, I felt thankful for this brief connection.

That evening, as I watched the sun set from the deck of our boat, I thought about the student and his candor. He said that as an economist, he would rather do a good job with a straightforward task than a mediocre job with a complex task, and that this was an ongoing challenge for someone looking for relationships between numbers and formulas. We had talked about how much less predictable fluid situations and contexts are. I watched the sun set with that in mind, knowing that there may or may not be colorful clouds surrounding the landscape. The sun might simply fall below the horizon. Many variables can impact the colors of the sunset. To me, every sunset and every sunrise is a mystery of nature.

This is the thing about mystery. If we follow our deepest desire, mystery is inevitable. We are not often given desires that are fulfilled simply. Our deepest desires invite us into a desert, into a jungle, into a forest. We are invited into a journey where we can't see the destination. This journey can be very lonely, and most often there is no money-back guarantee that our desire will reach fulfillment. Desire and mystery dance within us. We open our eyes to gaze at the horizon, and we close our eyes in exhaustion, perpetually reaching through mystery toward that which we are called to in our deep desire. Sometimes we can hear the song, and sometimes we can't, and we still continue on.

Mystery is by its very nature unknowable. If we choose to find and follow our deepest desire, if we choose to be the "most ourselves" that we can be, the outcome is never predictable. We can make a good guess, but we can't know. It is the desire itself that propels us through the uncertainty and the fear and the pain that lurks within the mystery we must enter. We tolerate the mystery in order to know the fulfillment of desire, or even to barely touch the deepest desire in our hearts. In the pursuit of desire and in the midst of mystery, we exchange our discomfort for hope.

The world we live in today teaches us that mystery is the enemy, that we should know all the answers, that even our phones contain more information than our brains. In my work as a psychiatrist, mystery has been an everyday companion. The minds of human beings are a mystery. We are learning more about the brain each decade, and we have the ability to influence neurochemical and neurophysiological processes. We create hypotheses about discomfort and suffering and do our best to offer what relief we can to the people who come seeking help.

I have always held a healthy respect for what we don't know, what we can't know, and what our patients may not know. Whether I saw a first grader with hyperactivity, a teenager with depression, a young adult with psychotic symptoms, or an older adult with anxiety, the pain of each one touched me beyond my psychiatric responsibility. I could "do all the right things" as a physician, and still my patient would suffer. When one would ask, "How long until I feel better?" I would search my heart for the best answer. Most often, I didn't know. Many times, relief could appear within a few weeks or even days. Yet there were times when months of treatment would barely make a dent in someone's experience. There were times when "treatment as usual" would not suffice. These were the times of mystery, and it was often a patient's own desire for healing that sustained them until they felt better.

As a physician, I became well acquainted with both desire and mystery. Similarly, in my spiritual direction practice, people often come to see me bearing both the desire for a closer and clearer connection with the Holy and the not-knowing of the mystery that travels with this deep desire. As humans, we are offered both desire and mystery in the same breath every day of our lives. I spent years witnessing this movement in others, and in this book, I share my own experiences with desire and mystery in the domains of love and intimacy, work and vocation, birth and parenting, grace and the Holy, wholeness and healing, creativity and creating, and finally, death and letting go.

One facet of this movement of desire and mystery remains: that of belonging, or community. I believe that belonging can bridge the gap that lies between desire and mystery. I believe that community, in all its different appearances, carries us through this journey and completes the trinity of our spiritual experience. Without belonging, this book would not exist. Without community, we would write but have no readers.

Today, back home from our river cruise, I lay in savasana at the end of my yoga class at my church, and I breathe my prayers for all these mysteries. For the frightened children separated from parents at our border, for the student in Heidelberg, for the young jazz musicians playing right outside our yoga classroom in a summer jazz workshop, for the unknown futures of all of these bright and beloved young people, and for ourselves.

May we be brave enough to enter the mystery, to consent to and allow ourselves to face the unknown and the unknowable. May we remember that our deepest desire is our touchstone to all that brings us life and love. May we welcome the opportunity to belong and to join in community and common humanity, carrying hope in the darkness of night and carrying peace in the light of day.

Chapter 4

BELONGING

Today, I am sitting on a bed in Taos, New Mexico. I am in an adobe structure with a ceiling supported by *vigas*, bare wooden rafters. As I look out of my window through lace curtains, I see morning sunlight falling on the mesa of Taos Pueblo. As I write, I am aware of how many ways I experience belonging. I understand "belonging" to connote relationships and community. I see belonging as the third movement in my exploration of desire and mystery. Belonging can be a bridge between the sweetness of our deep desires and the fear of our own mysteries. I find my own courage in belonging, and it supports me through both desire and mystery.

My own understanding of desire grew as I came to understand the holiness of this deep longing within us. That instead of being something to resist, desire is something to embrace. My experience with mystery was that it too was an enemy, that I was supposed to find and know the right answers to the questions of life. Mystery reminds us that certainty is scarce and that our need to know can erode our capacity to tolerate ambiguity. Mystery teaches us to live in the middles and the not-yets of life. We learn that we cannot control everything, or maybe anything, and yet control is our metric of success. As adults, we might resist both desire and mystery. In the face of these ambiguities that hinder our pursuit of our deepest desires, belonging can ease the way. But how?

I am not a natural joiner. I am introverted and prefer smaller social groups to larger ones. I also resist being labeled or pigeonholed, and this has been true for most of my life. As a shy child, joining a group like the Camp Fire Girls meant that I had to engage socially with other girls, even after a whole day of school. I liked the precepts of the Camp Fire Girls, but the actual meetings exhausted me. Even today, I appreciate boundaries at parties or other social events, and I like to know that I can leave and go home if the noise, activity, and energy level become uncomfortable for me. It is easier for me to be in quieter environments, and I like to spend time alone. I have learned to navigate my introverted perspective, and for me, being the life of any party is not essential. The party itself, however, is.

We need to come to the party. We need to be at the funeral, the wedding, the baby shower, the birthday party. We are wired for connection. As newborns, we would die without belonging. Babies grow because they belong to a family that feeds and takes care of them. Children grow as they expand their world beyond family to school and friends. Adults grow if they reach out and choose to allow belonging in their own lives. It is both who and how we are, and in today's world, our belonging is endangered. Our technology threatens belonging even as it offers a virtual alternative, an alternative that reinforces itself by eliciting dopamine responses in our brains. Our culture in its polarization discourages belonging to ourselves, to each other, to the Holy. We may know artificial belonging, but our wells of face-to-face relationship and community are so often dry.

Even as an introvert and someone who often resists affiliation, my greatest sources of joy and strength have been my experiences in community. I have iconic memories of specific groups that changed my life. These experiences are like pearls on a necklace for me, treasures close to my heart.

During college, I worked summers at YMCA conference centers, most often at the YMCA Blue Ridge Assembly in Black Mountain, North Carolina. The summer between high school and college was my first "real job." I worked with 100 other college students to support the conference activity at the center, setting up meeting spaces, staffing lobby areas to assist guests, and serving as a counselor for child care. I only knew one other staffer at the beginning of the summer, but by the end, I cherished my colleagues. It was a golden summer in the balance between childhood and adulthood, and we were gloriously free to be ourselves together. In a new way, I learned that I could be loved for who I am. I belonged to the Blue Ridge staff, and this is a connection that is still alive almost fifty years later.

A few years after I graduated from college, I joined the Jesuit Volunteer Corps, a young adult volunteer organization that places applicants in social justice-related work opportunities and in geographical communal living. This experience took me across the country where I knew no one to live with six strangers and to coordinate a free inner-city clinic. It also opened the door to my medical career by supporting my vocational discernment process. This belonging was both local with my own household and more broadly across the east coast with over 100 other volunteers. We gathered quarterly as a large group to reflect on our experiences and to celebrate together. Even when I flew home to Texas for the holidays, I would feel homesick for my Washington, D.C. housemates. Some of these relationships have been sustained over the years, and I know that seeing any of these friends would bring me great joy. In this belonging and community, I learned how to be who I am, and I made decisions that changed the course of my life. I learned about conflict as we argued and grieved together and about devotion as we loved and nurtured each other.

Not too long after my husband and I became Episcopalians and our five-year-old daughter was baptized, we became part of what some of us called "house church" and others of us called "home group." We were one of six families in our church who met monthly in each other's homes. We would eat, socialize, and often participate in a book study or watch a video series. We learned and shared together and would end by praying together. Our kids were all about the same age. We celebrated holidays and became close friends over the years. These were the families we trusted to care for our kids if something unexpected came up. These were the families who stood with us as we cared for and said goodbye to aging parents. These were the families we vacationed with and whose kids also became friends with each other. Families would move in and out of the group, but we knew that the others were there for support. This was and is intentional belonging, intentional community that let us practice what was preached in church. We listened to each other and offered sanctuary as a community. This belonging helped our small family build relationships where we lived and worshiped, forming friendships that have persisted over many years.

Every month, I sit with a group of women at my church at the twilight hour. We gather and settle into a quiet room upstairs. We begin with a few moments of quiet, a brief guided meditation, perhaps a poem or quote, and a prayer. We pass a stone heart around the circle, and the woman holding the heart speaks or passes, sharing whatever she feels led to voice. There is always enough time for everyone who wants to share to do so. We finish by praying together for each other and ourselves and the world. Although some women come in and out, this group has been gathering for six years. It is a private space and time filled with grace. There is no crosstalk and we don't "fix" each other, but as we listen, we might put a hand on our heart, wipe away a tear, or simply smile or nod as the woman talks. The ages of the women have ranged from the 20's to the 80's. This group, this community, is one of my most treasured belonging spaces. We are sisters of the spirit, and love abounds here.

Despite all the good that community brings, there can be a dark side of belonging. Affiliative groups who demand loyalty and obedience can begin naively and end in tragedy and disaster. The power of community can be used for good or for evil. In our world, it is not always easy to tell what any single group might be offering. Part of my drive to write this book is to reclaim the Holy in our lives that is grace. To speak to the profane and perverse caricatures of religion that cause pain and suffering in the name of Jesus and other holy ones. I hate political, religious, social, or governmental polarization with hidden agendas that eliminate humanity, that invite us to belonging with the goal of separating us from each other. We have to be wise as we search for our affiliation. Community is powerful and can heal or destroy with equal efficacy.

Belonging to ourselves, to our loved ones, to the Holy is how we learn that we are loved. Without knowing love, it is hard to understand how the traumas of this life can be met with courage and grace. Holy belonging that honors the individual and cherishes human dignity for all can change anything and everything. When we know this belonging, the holiness and wholeness that arise from the strength of love and the anger of injustice, then we are supported and freed as we follow our deepest desire, and then we are sustained as we enter the mysteries with faith and hope. This can be our path, if we choose. This is only one path, but all roads lead to universal redemption here.

May we be "wise as serpents and innocent as doves" (Matthew 10:16) as we seek and choose belonging in our hearts and in our lives. May we not fear anger but welcome it as our energy for reclaiming what has been lost, what might have never been at all. May we know the deep connection of belonging and community every day of our lives, and may we always remember that when we open to desire and to mystery, we are never alone.

LOVE

Chapter 5

LOVE

When many people hear the word "desire," their first thought is "love." Love is indeed related to desire in our common consciousness. Love is such a big concept. We love our spouses, and we love ice cream. We love our children, and we love Facebook posts. Love is a good place to start when exploring desire, mystery, and belonging because it is perhaps our most universal longing. Dr. Sigmund Freud, an early psychoanalytic pioneer, taught that "to love and to work" were the most basic of human prerequisites for happiness and health. Without love, infants literally fail to thrive. Love is an accessible gateway into our exploration, and love might be the easiest way to begin this story.

In **First Loves** I take a look at my very early idealized love experiences—not familial, but social. These were the earliest beginnings of my understanding of romantic love, the love of fairy tales and happily-ever-afters. Mine was not an easy journey, and this story is one that was easier to keep to myself as a young girl. I found early love risky. It was also the beginning of my understanding of how gender impacted the outcome of lots of possibilities. Being a girl seemed to require secret knowledge and secret rules. My journey had a little bit of a rocky beginning. I was loved in my family, but my shyness kept me timid in affairs of the heart until adolescence.

Bob is the happy story of falling in love with my husband. I was a late bloomer, and our path was unique, at least to us. We were perhaps an unlikely pair, yet in many ways, we could not have been more naturally matched. This journey has been for me a shining tale of desire, mystery, and belonging that puts the fairy tales I learned as a child to shame. I know well how lucky I am, how lucky we are, and I love telling our story.

Finally, **Agape and Common Humanity** broadens the context of love to a wider and deeper landscape. We are part of a greater human family that spans continents. Agape, one of the Greek words for love, connotes the love of humans for other humans beyond our immediate family and community. Agape is also our response to the call of a God who loves unconditionally, to love others in return without condition or requirements to be like us or to earn our love. Love for love's sake. Without thought for reciprocity. Holy love.

Desire calls us to love in all its ways. Sooner or later, we say yes and follow into the mystery of the unknown land of love. We finally arrive at a new territory when we agree to belong and invite others to join us, whether in our own community or across the planet. We reach out in inclusion and in grace. Love has so much to offer and to teach. May we open our hearts as we journey forward.

Chapter 6

First Loves

It starts with desire. It was, in fact, a boy who caused my first problem in school. I was in the first grade, in a special class for younger kids who were ready to start school early. We were all five years old, rather than the usual six years old. Our teacher was very young, and our principal was very tall and scary. I was quiet most of the time and only spoke when I had to.

I remember a lot of worksheets throughout the day. I tended to finish quickly and then sit at my desk. We weren't allowed to read or otherwise do anything except sit quietly. I had really looked forward to starting school, but it turned out to be really boring. I spent a lot of the time daydreaming and making up stories. When I got home, I would "write" the stories and draw pictures. Both my parents loved to read, and my mother would help me, which is how I learned to write actual words. Most of my class was still learning the alphabet, but I had been to kindergarten and already knew how to read.

The saving grace of first grade was a little boy in my class. He was cute and smiled all the time. Everyone wanted to play with him during recess. He was as friendly as I was shy. I watched him from afar, making up stories in my mind about him. I daydreamed that he liked me.

One day, he got in trouble for some misbehavior. Our teacher made him stand in the corner in the back of the room. I felt so sad for him, and while we did that morning's worksheets, I kept squirming at my desk and turning around to look at him. Finally, I raised my hand to ask if I might go and sharpen my pencil. The teacher said yes, so I walked to the back of the room to use the pencil sharpener. Everyone was still working at their desks, and the teacher was reading something at her desk at the front of the classroom. All of a sudden, I found myself walking over to the corner where the cute boy stood. I quickly reached out and kissed him very fast and very softly on the back of his neck. He immediately screamed and shrieked, and for a moment, it wasn't clear to anyone except me what had happened. Our teacher told the boy to go back to his seat. She told me to stand in the corner. I was mortified. I had never been in trouble before. I stood there, my face burning bright red. My eyes filled with tears. My stomach felt like I would throw up. I thought I might die, standing there in the corner. I was only five years old.

After a bit, my teacher told me to go back to my seat. I stared at the floor as I walked back. I then stared at my desk until the end of the school day. No one said anything to me. I felt invisible and ashamed at the same time. I didn't tell anyone at home, but I knew one thing for sure: It would be a very long time before I would kiss anyone again.

I grew up in a home with three younger sisters. It was a very girly place. My father was there, and while I loved spending time with him, he would often read, play chess, watch baseball on TV, or listen to music. My mother made our clothes, cooked dinner every night, and spent a lot of time driving us to three different schools and various after-school activities, like piano lessons, dance lessons, and Camp Fire Girls. I really didn't know many boys except my cousins, who lived several states away. I saw them once a year in the summer. I loved my father and felt very close to him, but boys themselves were a mystery to me.

And yet, I secretly loved boys. I loved comparing boys with brown eyes to boys with blue eyes. I couldn't decide which I loved more. I loved looking at boys' hands. And their hair. I kept track in my mind of all the times I would "accidentally" brush against the cutest boys in the hall or in the cafeteria or at recess. This most minimal of touches thrilled me. I knew boys were different from me. I decided I would want an older boyfriend. Every year, I picked out a secret boyfriend in my class and told myself stories about him and about our love together. Every year, I wrote his name in my diary, over and over again. All of this was my own secret, in my own mind.

One day in sixth grade, my then-current secret crush, a brown-haired, brown-eyed boy who played the guitar and smiled a lot, said hi to me at recess. I froze inside, but I tried to act "normal," and I said hi back to him. He handed me a note, smiled, and walked away. I unfolded the note and read, in his scrawling boyish handwriting, "Will you trade discs with me?" That year, both boys and girls wore silver discs engraved with our names on chains around our necks. When we chose and were chosen as boyfriends and girlfriends, we exchanged discs to announce our new relationships. My heart beat fast as I reached up to hold the disc I wore. I lifted the necklace off over my head and walked over to him on the playground. I reached out my hand, holding out my disc. He looked at me, not under-standing. He smiled at me kindly but didn't say anything else. I gave him back the note he had written. He looked at the note and then at the ground, digging his toe into the dirt for a second. Then he whispered in my ear, "I meant, will you trade desks with me? I want to sit where you sit." And all of a sudden, I knew. He wanted to sit next to the girl who sat next to me. I was embarrassed and afraid I might cry, but he was kind. He put his hand gently on my arm. I felt the same little goosebump tickle I felt every time I bumped into or brushed against a boy.

I looked in his eyes and whispered back, "Yes." After recess, we exchanged seats, and he went on to have a happy and long relation-ship with my seat neighbor. And he also went on to be kind to me whenever he saw me. I learned, albeit painfully, that I could be rejected and life would go on. That I could enjoy my desire and not have to get everything I wanted. That desire in itself was mine to know and mine to keep, a treasure in my sixth-grade heart.

As a teenager, I grew to be less shy. I had a curious mind and close girlfriends. In junior high, boys sought me out to "talk." As my academic achievement became more important, I found my comfort zone. I helped others with their homework. I got to know boys as friends in church youth groups, at the YMCA, and in my classes. I still wanted an older boyfriend. In high school, I had a close group of friends, most of whom dated each other over the years. It was in college that I wandered into more traditional romantic territory, but even then, the ethos of the time supported casual relationships, and every guy I dated was my platonic friend first. Guys no longer seemed foreign to me. As a psychology student in the seventies, "authentic relationships" were emphasized as a part of healthy living. I spent many hours in group settings, both educational and recreational, where I saw many men speak of personal growth. Sensitive men were attractive. I had a succession of what I remember as "relationships of interest," none of which were particularly intimate and none of which lasted very long. I had several boyfriends who I loved, but we mostly eventually separated from our romantic relationships as friends.

What I didn't do for many years was really, truly fall in love. Not beyond the comforting closeness of friendship and "making out." I wasn't ready for grown up love... but I thrived on desire. I dreamed of marrying a loving man, of having a family and a home, of being cherished. After college, however, I would move far away from home and feel called to a career in medicine. Since I hadn't taken any pre-requisite classes for medical school, this would be a long journey and preparing would take years.

The desire would abide, and the mystery of my future was just around the corner. I would eventually fall in love and marry a beloved husband and make a home with him and our cherished child, but that was a long time away. Desire was a flame inside me. I saw it then as all the boys I loved. What I didn't know was how it would evolve—that it was all of that, and so much more. At the time, I held my own heart close. I was about to enter the mystery, and it would be belonging itself—community—that would open the future to me and bring back desire in the form of love, in all its light and longing, to the very center of my life.

Chapter 7

BOB

I fell in love with my husband the way I fall in love with geography.

A place settles into my bloodstream, and its smells settle into my limbic system. My brain then recognizes aromas from years past, and I remember what that place looked like, sounded like, tasted like. I remember how I felt there. I remember what and who I loved there.

The other thing about falling in love this way is that it is mostly unconscious. Seeds are planted deep inside me, in a place of openness, and it can be many years before I realize how filled I am with love for this or that place. I suddenly find myself homesick for these places and their parts... sunlight in New Mexico, twilight in Galveston. Time collapses, and I desire and yearn for the light that calls me.

This kind of falling in love—this desire—means that I am already home long before I know I've arrived.

When I met Bob, I had been living in Galveston for almost four years. I was three months away from graduating from medical school. He moved to Galveston from Cincinnati that spring to work at the church I belonged to. This church was served by Franciscan friars, priests who followed the way of St. Francis of Assisi. These men loved Jesus, lived simply, and worked for social justice. They took vows of poverty, chastity, and obedience. They ministered to homeless persons and refugees as well as schools and congregations. I had become friends with several of the Galveston friars, and they told me that spring that Bob was coming. I learned that he had a mental health counseling background in addition to his ministry. I was expecting to move to Washington, D.C. in the next few months to begin my psychiatry internship, so in the beginning, Bob was someone I thought I would know perhaps only briefly.

The day I met him, I stopped in the church office for something. I lived in a nearby apartment, and I was active in several church programs. I was wearing a blue sundress, and it was a sunny spring day, the kind where light dances and sparkles on the Gulf of Mexico, which is walking distance from almost anywhere in Galveston. I saw Bob in the office, and a staff person introduced us. Bob was tall and had brown hair and bright blue eyes. He was dressed in shorts and already tan from running daily on the Galveston sea wall. He smiled at me, and soon we were talking about the Enneagram, a personality typology. I had just finished reading a book about the personality types in this theory. I found it interesting but was resistant to categorizing myself in this system. He asked me what type I thought I was. The types are numbered 1-9. I remember laughing and saying, "I'm not in that book! I'm a 10!"

He laughed too, and said, "Then you're a 4! I'm a 4 too!" When I got home, I looked up the 4 type. He was right. I was a type 4. Enneagram 4s resist being categorized. I think that may have been the moment that something of Bob began slowly seeping into me. He saw me, and he heard me. Even though I was about to leave and move to another part of the country.

I drove my dad's Honda Civic to Washington, D.C. after medical school graduation. My used red Ford Pinto had just died after needing a third new transmission. My internship at Georgetown, like all medical internships, was exhilarating and exhausting and consisted of months of being on call at the hospital every third night. The first night I worked, the second night I slept, the third night I would do laundry or buy groceries or stare at a book. Previously, I had lived in D.C. for two years, so I knew the city and had some friends there. It was during my internship that I transformed into a "real doctor." This changed me in ways that would take years for me to realize.

I had a lot of support, and I worked very hard. I learned to make diagnoses that were lifesaving for patients, but at the same time, I became physically and mentally exhausted. I never had time to see my friends, and the three D.C. blizzards in January made me yearn for Galveston as I never had before. This Southern girl with thin blood almost froze. I didn't even own a winter coat! I wanted to go home. I called the residency training director at my medical school and asked if there might be an open space for me in the second-year program. He told me I would be welcome and no interview was required. So, that June, I drove my dad's Civic back to Galveston to begin the second year of my residency there.

Bob was still in Galveston and now the pastor of my church. For the next four years, while I completed adult and child psychiatry residencies, we were friends. He was a wonderful priest and a creative preacher. He reminded me of St. Francis in that he appeared unencumbered by the worries that burdened most people, including me. Bob basically seemed to be a faithful optimist. He expected that all things would turn out well. As someone whose professional education taught hypervigilance, I found this internal assurance mesmerizing. As we came to know each other more closely, I learned that he could worry and he could get tired, but that mostly he was free from concerns. He lived within a deep joy that to me was a constant light. I learned the geography of Bob the way I had learned other landscapes: silently, deeply, and unconsciously—the way I fall in love. At the time, I had no thought of romantic love with Bob as I was too busy with my work in residency training, and my own faith understood well that falling in love was not an option for either of us. We were Roman Catholics, and he had taken a vow of celibacy. We were true, close friends on that island. The love of friendship was strong and nurturing. We would walk on the beach on Sunday afternoons and drink Irish coffee in the evenings. We talked about everything and nothing. He was my safe harbor.

As I was finishing my residency, five years after we met, Bob told me he was taking a leave of absence from the priesthood. He was in a place of discernment and needed time to consider his next steps. I was surprised but supportive. I had accepted a faculty position at the medical school, which meant that I would be staying in Galveston rather than accepting an attractive job offer with a group practice in Austin.

I had always hoped to return to Austin, where I had studied as an undergraduate, but I had a sense that I was being invited to stay put for the time being. I moved to a bigger apartment in Galveston and bought all new furniture, and Bob rented a small apartment near me and accepted a counseling position in a local social services agency.

It was then, and only then, that the doors of our minds began to gradually open to the possibility of a different relationship. Our friendship slowly became a tender love that would lead us to a life together, to becoming a family. We traveled to New Mexico that fall and walked all through the Taos Pueblo. We visited my family in east Texas at Thanksgiving. Bob invited me to spend Christmas with his family in Cincinnati. Our families welcomed us and adjusted to this new life and love growing within us.

Some of my more intuitive friends wondered about this new love before I did. My hope had always been to preserve my friendship with Bob even as I was unsure where our romantic relationship was going. I had been in committed relationships in the past, but I had never been close to marriage. I was basically married to my vocation, to being a psychiatrist, and on good days, married to my faith. It seems that my friends knew better and asked me questions I couldn't answer. The truth was that I wasn't sure where we were headed. I knew that Bob could—and might—return to active priesthood at the end of his leave of absence. I left room for this possibility even as I felt closer and closer to him. In my work, I tried to help families understand risks and benefits of decisions involving treatment. In my own life, I found myself in a context where what I could do—all I could do—was live day by day and enjoy the present. But when the time came, when we knew it was right, Bob and I entered into engagement with amazement and a sense of awe.

Six months later, we were married in Galveston with our families and best friends present. Weddings make me nervous, and this one was no different—except that this one was mine, and I already knew the man I was marrying. I knew him in my heart and in my soul. I knew the light in his eyes and the energy in his step. I knew that

I would recognize this love all of my life. It felt like both a miracle and the most natural process ever. It felt like coming home.

I fell in love with Bob, the way I fall in love with geography. I know that this love, like all love, is rooted in the Holy, and I give thanks for the sweetness of all our todays and the light of all our tomorrows. He is deep desire for me. I cannot imagine being without him, and I believe that the Holy holds both our hearts together. May our love be a sign and a sacrament as we face outward together, and may we always know gratitude and peace in the love that is our home.

Chapter 8

AGAPE AND COMMON HUMANITY

Love as experienced in desire, mystery, and belonging is impossible
to contain neatly. Love is a word that has meant so many things in
the universe we live in that it can sound trite and easily dismissed.
The Greeks spoke of *eros* as romantic or sexual love and *philos* as
friendship, or the love of companions. I've shared stories about eros,
including my ill-fated earliest romantic loves and how I met my
husband. I will also share stories about philos, including stories
about my daughter, my friends, and my family. However, I can't
think of writing about love in the arenas of desire, mystery, and
belonging without exploring a third Greek word for love: *agape.*

Agape is used in Christian contexts to name the kind of love that
God has for humans. Agape is a love that is unconditional and independent of any external situation. It means love for all, and to me,
agape's main difference from eros and philos is that agape means love
for the other. Agape is us loving each other and loving the stranger
next door with the same love that God has for us and for all of
creation. This does not come naturally, as it is easy to see in the world
around us. It has never come naturally.

I believe in and love God. I am a Christian, and I cringe each day
as I read of "Christians" in the news, especially the Christians that are
mixing political and religious metaphors. Part of what draws me to
write about spirituality is my own desire to reclaim a broader context
for those of us who love and follow Jesus. There is indeed a lot of room
at the table. Our world feels lost in aggression, lost in ridicule, lost in
everything that is not love. If desire, mystery, and belonging support
anything, it is agape love. Love for humanity and love for our planet.

I believe that agape can be a feeling of the heart. But it doesn't have to be. The essential component seems to me to be the "undeserved" quality, the non-transactional nature of this kind of love.

Agape does not have to be earned. It is not transactional. It is not really human love, in my mind, but rather a love derived from the Holy. I believe that we walk side by side with holy realities. I believe that the world we live in is both seen and unseen, which means we as humans are both seen and unseen. There is a love that moves beyond romance, beyond familiarity, beyond bonds of family by birth or by choice. This is agape. This is why a wedding on reality TV can make me weepy. It might be contrived and manipulative, and yet there is something universal in a million different flavors that touches us when we witness goodness. When we experience spontaneous peace. When we recognize the human condition in our own hearts and offer grace to someone else.

What I know is that agape seems to be an endangered species of love. Christians may and do participate in what are called "agape meals"—seasonal celebrations that may include ritual eating of beloved traditional foods and to which all are invited. I have attended these occasions, and they can be delightful. The challenge of sustaining agape comes after the meal is finished. In today's world, where is compassion? Where is empathy? It matters in the small moments we share as well as at the voting booth, and it feels increasingly hard to find.

I find myself recasting the vision of agape into a vision of "common humanity." In the moments I sense agape, I reflect on common humanity. In the most basic biology, we are all the same. For me, the recognition of common humanity infused with agape love is the love I aspire to in my own life. I believe that desire, mystery, and belonging can and do support us as we walk this path of love:

- Desire opens the door to what we value most, to how we want to live.
- Mystery reminds us that we are human and that no specific outcome can ever be guaranteed.
- Belonging invites us to walk together and to be each other's eyes in the times we find it hard to see.

I find that both agape and common humanity are present at sites of devotion. I visited the Basilica of Our Lady of Guadalupe in Mexico City twice during my years as a psychiatry resident. Both times, I went with a church group. At the basilica, pilgrims are invited to ride a slowly moving sidewalk that passes by the *tilma* (cloak) of St. Juan Diego, where Mary's likeness appeared in the legend. I found myself in tears as I looked around the huge church. The sight of so many people praying together in the same place opened a door in my own heart. What surprised me was not so much seeing the tilma itself, it was the presence of devotion that spoke to me of agape here, of common humanity here. I learned to look for signs of devotion that would be the gateway to this love, this agape, this common humanity. Outside the church, we slowly climbed steps up a hill, where a priest waited at the top to bless us with red roses dipped in holy water. Here, we prayed for the whole world, seen and unseen. The experience of grace was palpable. The truest miracle at Guadalupe was the devotion of sisters and brothers I will never know, devotion that was more about faithfulness than about any specific path.

Years later, I visited Jerusalem. This time, I was also with a church group, along with my husband and daughter. The flight across the Atlantic from Toronto to Tel Aviv was long. The cabin was warm, and I was too excited to sleep. When I got up to use the restroom, I noticed men laying rugs on the cabin floor. When I came out of the restroom, I saw the men praying on their rugs, all facing the same direction, the front of the plane. I carefully stepped around them on my way back to my seat. Some hours later, I woke from napping to a couple of babies crying. I looked in the aisle next to us, and I saw several men standing and donning *tefillin*[1] and moving into the aisle, where they began softly *davening*[2]. I could see the sun rising through the windows by their seats. I had never seen this kind of devotion—

---

1 Tefillin or phylacteries, is a set of small black leather boxes containing scrolls of parchment inscribed with verses from the Torah. Tefillin are worn by observant adult Jews during weekday morning prayers.

2 (in Judaism) to recite the prescribed liturgical prayers.

from Muslims or Jews or Christians—in such a secular environment as an airplane. Witnessing these prayers heightened my awareness of devotion, and spending the long night all together in a tight space reminded me of agape, of common humanity, and of my desire to know the peace of God for myself and for the world.

A few days later, I would lay my hand on the Western Wall and pray for peace with a strength I had never known. Again, the experiences of desire, mystery, and belonging supported me as I approached a Love with no name, surrounded by common humanity. It happened again standing on the Haram esh-Sharif and the Al Aqsa Compound hill, the holy site of Islam, as I smiled at women walking by, only their eyes visible to me. It also happened in Bethlehem as I was kneeling to reach and touch the silver star on the floor in the church of the Nativity, the site where it is said that Jesus was born. I was overwhelmed again and again by devotion and the common humanity that speaks of hope—of hope for peace and of love for all of creation.

More recently, I also visited the town of Assisi in Umbria, Italy. I have been there twice and will visit again in a few months. Assisi is the home of St. Francis, the saint that many associate with the blessing of animals. The movie "Brother Sun Sister Moon" is his story, made by Franco Zeffirelli in 1972. I saw this movie in college and was deeply moved by the lives of Francis and Clare, who both founded religious orders in the 1200s. Assisi is beautiful and, I think, the most peaceful place I have ever been. There is a gentleness in the air that whispers of love, of agape. The spirituality of Francis embraced all of creation. It embraced lepers who were the "other" of his time. It embraced delight as well as sorrow. It was a devotion to all love. For me, Assisi holds desire and mystery and belonging all in one place and across the ages. I sat at the tomb of Francis and wrote these words:

> "This love, this desire, blooms like the sunflowers across the Umbrian valley. This desire of Francis for Jesus was a passion that exploded into love for the whole world. For me, all love comes from the Holy, from the place inside where we don't even know. All we know is love and joy and wholeness. A love that doesn't die when we do.
> Love all you can.

Remember these cobblestone streets.
Remember smiling eyes and arms that reach.
Kindness and grace and mercy
And light,
Always, the gift of light.
A new calculus of suffering
Enveloped in a greater whole of light and grace.
These words: only love, creation, humans, the Holy.
We are not separate.
Peace is the way."

When I need to remember common humanity, I love to remember Assisi—the spaciousness of the air and the sounds of birds singing. I will hold its beautiful clear light in my heart for the rest of my days.

Love is impossible to contain neatly. It is impossible to contain at all. The wildness of agape ensures, I believe, that this broadest and deepest love is not dead. "If we want to know God, follow our deepest desire," said St. Bonaventure. It is never too late to love like this, to live in agape, to devote ourselves to honoring common humanity.

May we believe our desire when it calls to us from deep within, and may we believe that deep calls to deep. May we believe that the mysteries around us encourage us to grow, and may we believe that this is our vocation. May we believe that common humanity is truly the only humanity we have, and may we believe that belonging brings us home to agape and to all love.

WORK AND VOCATION

Chapter 9

WORK AND VOCATION

After love, the next most basic human experience might be work. "What do you do?" is the question that arises quickly when we meet a new person. We either ask this of our new acquaintance, or they ask us. What we almost always want to know is what kind of work someone does. How do they earn a living? Or do they earn a living? We are socialized to stratify those we meet based on their earning practice and potential. Here, social becomes professional, and the reverse is true as well. What is often lost is the reality of "vocation"—literally "call" from the Latin *vocatio*. Sometimes our work is "just a job," and other times we feel called to a certain profession. Clergy are commonly understood to be "called," but they are not the only ones. Teachers, nurses, physicians, artists, writers, actors, and even politicians can believe they are called to their choice of profession and see it as their vocation. This was my path to medicine, an unexpected journey that involved surprising desires, mysteries, and belonging along the way.

The first story, **Called to Become a Healer**, traces my path from studying psychology as an undergraduate, to medical school, and finally to psychiatry as a vocation. Much like the story of falling in love with my husband, this path emerged for me out of *desires* that became symbols, *mysteries* that asked me to have faith and believe in my own sense of mission, and *belonging* that drew me into the medical community in my own community.

The second story, **The Day I Forgot How To Read**, comes from the first year of my psychiatry residency, my internship. It speaks to my early experience with and understanding of the mind-body-spirit connection that would later become so essential to my career expanding beyond psychiatry. Internships are legendary. They become stories that are retold throughout any physician's career, and mine was no different. Times have changed, and parameters are now in place for physicians in training to help preserve life-work balance. However, at the time, I fell into a deep hole as an intern, and the consequences were severe.

The final story, **Practicing Medicine**, looks back at my own medical career with an eye to the influence of desire, mystery, and belonging along the way. I evolved as an administrative psychiatrist over the years for a number of reasons. I expanded my understanding of healing and reached into new realms of experience as I grew older. It was not easy to retire from my "job," but I am learning that I am still a healer —still serving my vocation—and pray to remain so all of my life. I hope to never stop exploring new vistas of healing and wholeness.

These stories explore my work and vocation as a physician, but you can draw parallels to any vocation. How we discern our desire in the context of a vocational call, how we navigate the mysteries, ambiguities, threats, and hardships of our chosen work (for there are always risks), and how we reach out to colleagues and develop the networks that support the work that we do and help make our efforts meaningful and sustainable—all of this impacts our journey and our response to the call that first beckoned us.

Chapter 10

CALLED TO BECOME A HEALER

In 1978, I was twenty-four years old with a bachelor's degree in psychology. I was working for the state rehabilitation commission in Austin and had grown bored with my job as a disability examiner. I yearned to do something more exciting and "meaningful." I applied to join the Jesuit Volunteer Corps (JVC), an organization much like the Peace Corps, and I was accepted and assigned to Washington, D.C. My family was surprised and supportive—and probably very worried.

I resigned my salaried position and moved across the country to live in inner-city D.C. with six other volunteers in a creaky, ancient, four-story, red brick townhouse near Thomas Circle. My job was to be one of two coordinators for Zacchaeus Medical Clinic, a free clinic supported by the church across the street, Luther Place Church. The clinic had an almost totally volunteer staff and was funded by donations. It had been founded years earlier by the Community for Creative Non-Violence (CCNV), and a few CCNV members continued to volunteer. My partner coordinator was a nun, a Sister of Notre Dame de Namur, from Philadelphia. The clinic was open for patients to be seen by a physician three times each week (Tuesday and Thursday evenings and Saturday mornings), and a physician assistant was present onsite during the weekdays. My coordinator partner and I oversaw and managed the clinic sessions, scheduled volunteers, ordered medications and other supplies, obtained lab supplies from the city health department, cleaned the clinic daily, and did whatever else needed to be done, including summoning police for the occasional waiting room brawl. Our volunteers were generous and gifted professionals and laypersons who served as physicians, nurses, laboratory technologists, and front desk staff. During this time, I fell in love with healthcare and with healing. My six housemates became like family very quickly, and I loved them fiercely.

As a new convert to the Roman Catholic church, I thought often about the connections between my JVC life and what might come next. I had no idea what I would do when my volunteer year ended. Since I didn't have a plan, I ended up staying for a second year as the JVC coordinator of Zacchaeus Clinic, again along with my coordinator partner. As Jesuit Volunteers, we were encouraged to see a spiritual director on a regular basis. I knew nothing about spiritual direction and was apprehensive about trying it, so I didn't during my first volunteer year. In the second year, I decided to try spiritual direction but sought out a Franciscan priest rather than a Jesuit, maybe to be sure of the boundaries and privacy I felt I needed. A couple of our clinic volunteers were Franciscan brothers and referred me to one of their community members.

When I went for the first time to the Franciscan monastery, I took the Metro subway train to Brookland Station and walked a few blocks to the monastery grounds and up a very long driveway. At the monastery door, an older friar wearing a brown habit belted at his waist with a white cord summoned my new spiritual director by ringing a series of bells. I was nervous. A few minutes later, a slender young priest with red hair appeared in blue jeans and a T-shirt to greet me.

Thus began my first spiritual direction relationship that very quickly focused my prayer on discernment. I began a new kind of private prayer, a more contemplative and meditative attempt. He encouraged me to pay attention to my dreams. Within a few months, and with his encouragement, I planned to go on a private weekend retreat at the Jesuit center in Wernersville, Pennsylvania. I visited him monthly, and he listened and supported my exploration.

It was on the retreat at Wernersville that I first heard clearly the call to study and practice medicine. The retreat center was silent and no one talked, even at meals. There were snacks and arts and crafts supplies and beautiful gardens and grounds. The very first night at the retreat center, I went to bed in my tiny, private, cell-like room and lay awake. It was so quiet that it was hard to fall asleep. I was accustomed to the city noises of trucks and police cars and prostitutes working in our inner-city neighborhood. I tossed and turned.

The second night, I had a series of seven dreams, all of which were lucid dreams. I knew that I was dreaming and remembered all of them. The fourth dream, the central dream that night, arrived in my awareness like a special delivery package.

> I am standing at the base of a high and rocky mountain. I start to climb up, but I find it very difficult. Just when I think I need to give up, all of a sudden, I am lifted up and fly through stars higher up the mountain. Eventually, I am set down and continue to climb. Again, I think of giving up as I am hot and so tired. Again, I am lifted up, flying through stars higher up the mountain. I am again placed on the mountain and keep climbing. For a third time, I want to stop. For a third and final time, I am lifted to fly through stars. However, this time, I am set down at the top of the mountain, where a small village sits. I am drawn to walk down the central road and come to a building in the village's center. It is a large white building, a hospital, with a cross on top. A star shines over the cross. I know that this is where I am called to be... both as a healer and a believer. And I know that I will have to start over and walk into the unknown to say yes. The words spoken to me in the dream were, "Through clouds, with heart, to stars."

The next morning, I made a collage of this dream in the retreat center's craft room. I would later take it home and hang it on the wall in my bedroom. Since this was a silent retreat, I simply kept this central dream in my knowing. That Sunday morning, I walked the retreat center grounds and found myself climbing a small hill and looking around at the landscape. It was February, and a cold winter wind was blowing. I could feel the bite through my coat. As I looked around at the bare trees, suddenly the sun came out from behind a cloud, and the wind stopped. Everything was quiet for a moment. I stood very still at the top of the hill and uttered the word, "Yes." Just yes. And when I came back to Washington, I began, with my spiritual director's help, to enter the process of discernment toward medical school.

Soon after the retreat, I was home with my housemates when a local Jesuit priest, Fr. Horace McKenna, came to visit us. Fr. McKenna was a retired, elderly Jesuit priest who had worked tirelessly all his life to build support systems for the poor, especially poor youths, in the Capitol Hill area in the context of ministry at St. Aloysius Catholic Church. Some thought he was a saint. Fr. McKenna was a mentor for our Jesuit Volunteer community. He was a very kind, bright, and humble man. At some point in the conversation with my housemates, he looked at me and said simply, "You should go to medical school." My housemates later told me, half-jokingly, that now I had no choice, that the counsel of Horace McKenna was as close as someone on earth could come to a direct message from God.

In that moment, I knew the invitation. I was called to become a healer. I was called to say yes to the climb. I was called to trust that I would be lifted when the journey was too hard. I was called to believe that I could fly. I was called through a dream to know in my bones that healing is holy. And I said yes. Yes to the dream, yes to the climb, and yes to the call.

Yes.

Chapter 11

THE DAY I FORGOT HOW TO READ

It was sometime in March—I don't remember when, exactly—but it was toward the end of my internship year in psychiatry. I had graduated from medical school in Galveston a year earlier and was based at a hospital in suburban Virginia, about thirty minutes' drive from my basement studio apartment on W Street in Washington, D. C. I was in a psychiatry internship program that would last for a year and included five months of internal medicine work, four on inpatient units, and one in the intensive care unit. Rotation sites changed each month. That month, something had already happened that had me worried. Normally, a team had two interns. However, I was placed on a team as the only intern, so there would be no days off for me that month.

I was being trained in psychiatry, but I needed a strong internal medicine background to be a good psychiatrist. I was ready and willing. This particular rotation would only be for a month, so I was compliant and cooperative. I had already survived three snowstorms in January. What could be worse than that?

So, reminding myself that all internships are torturous, I stepped up to this assignment and cheerfully doubled my stack of index cards, one for each patient. I stayed in the hospital on call the first night, slept the second night after thirty-six hours of work, and did my laundry and went to the grocery store on the third night. The next night, it would start all over again. While on call, I carried a pager and roamed the hospital responding to calls for everything from ordering Tylenol for a headache to pronouncing a patient dead. If a code was called, I helped out as asked. I kept track of all my patients, worked to admit new ones and discharge those who got better, and I fed information steadily to my resident, who then fed it to the chief resident and the attending physician.

One night, a little over halfway through the month of March, I was on call. My resident told me that a new patient was being transferred and flown to our hospital and that she would be my patient. She was from a notable Middle Eastern country, and she herself did not speak English. Before he could finish telling me about her, she arrived in a helicopter, and we ran to the emergency room to meet her.

I didn't leave her side for the next twelve hours. She had a horrible skin infection that was literally decaying flesh in her abdomen. Her kidneys were not working. All of her blood counts, red cells, white cells, and platelets were wildly abnormal. She had a cardiac arrhythmia and a high fever. And she was crying. An interpreter was present, and she told her story in a hesitating stutter, weeping quietly all the while. I reached out and held her hand.

She didn't let go. There were medical specialists evaluating her over the next few hours, ordering lab tests, other studies, and medication. She had orders from at least four different specialty departments. It was my job as the intern to track all the tests and, in those days before electronic medical records, to compile the results. As midnight approached, she and her chart went all over the hospital to different places: the lab, dialysis, x-ray, to name a few. She kept reaching out for my hand, so I held her hand with one of mine and held her chart with my other. It was a miracle that she was alive. She was only a little older than I was. My resident said he was going to take a nap, but I stayed with the patient. Somehow, all of the other patients in the hospital were inexplicably quiet that night. I stayed by her bedside and held her hand.

Hours later, my patient finally fell asleep. I ached in every muscle, and I was hungry and thirsty and needed to go to the bathroom. I eased my fingers out of hers. I walked to the nurses' station and could see the sky outside beginning to lighten. As I searched for the coffee pot, my pager went off. I recognized the call room extension where my resident had been napping. I called the number, and he sleepily said to me, "Don't forget to be ready to present our new patient in morning report at 8:00 am," and hung up.

I held the receiver in my hand. At that moment, my mind started to spin with thoughts of lab reports, history, response to dialysis, and chest x-ray films. In a few short hours, I would be expected to flawlessly recite all of this and more to a room filled with all the internal medicine staff, faculty, residents, and medical students. There was a senior faculty physician who moderated morning report, and when it was my team's turn to present, he would relentlessly question me, calling me "the shrink." He would yell if I answered a question wrong and laughed when I answered it right. I was afraid of him. I had two hours to assemble this presentation while still taking care of patients. My mouth was dry, and my heart began to race. I felt out of breath. I hated morning report, and I hated making mistakes even more. I knew that even though this patient's test results would not be ready, I would still be questioned about them. I would feel blamed for not having all the information even if it wasn't available to anyone yet. I sat there holding the receiver, and a nurse walked over, took the receiver out of my hand, and hung it up on the telephone base. She asked, "Are you okay?"

I was staring at a poster on the wall. I kept staring at it. I could see a picture on it and some black markings that I knew were letters, but I could not read the letters. I rubbed my eyes and shook my head. I still couldn't read the letters. I waited a moment. Finally, I looked up at the nurse and shook my head again. I whispered, "No. I can't read."

I learned how to read when I was four years old. I read the way other people breathe. Reading had always been my oxygen. But that early morning, I couldn't read anything. I had worked for a month earlier that year on a neurology unit, and I had seen all kinds of brain disorders. I looked at the nurse and said aloud, "I can't read. I don't know what to do. I can't go to morning report." My eyes teared up, and I blew my nose. I felt horribly, horribly ashamed. What was wrong with me?

The kind nurse suggested that I call the neurology resident on call. I knew him, as he was also working in the psychiatry department. I told her I couldn't read the numbers to dial the phone. She called him herself and explained my symptoms. He asked her to tell me to come to his office. I told her I didn't think I could read the signs to get there. She relayed this message to him and then handed me the phone. He asked me a few questions that I don't remember and then told me, "You know the way here, just stand up and walk."

As the sun rose, I walked carefully through the hospital to his office. My pager kept going off. I ignored it. The neurology resident was waiting for me in the doorway of his office. He invited me in and asked me to sit down. He looked carefully at me for a few seconds. Then he asked, "Did you sleep at all last night?"

I said, "No."

He asked, "Did you eat anything?"

"No."

"When was your last day off?"

"Last month. I can't have any days off this month."

"Why not? Where is the other intern on your team?"

"I'm the only one."

"Who is your resident?"

I told him, and we sat there together silently for a moment.

He picked up the phone on his desk and called the office of the department chief of psychiatry. When the secretary picked up, he said that he was coming there now and bringing me with him. By now, it was almost 8:00 am. I choked a little as I swallowed my threatening tears, and said, "But I have to present at morning report."

"Not today, you don't," he said.

I had no idea what would happen next. As we walked through the hospital to the psychiatry department, I thought that maybe this would be the end of my career. The career that had just barely started. Or maybe there was something wrong with me. Would that be my fault? What on earth was going to happen at morning report when I didn't show up? What would my resident do? What would the moderator say? Would they all hate me? Would anyone at all be worried?

And just as we arrived at the office of the chair of the psychiatry department, I stopped for a moment. I stood still. What if I really couldn't read anymore? What would life be if I couldn't read? How would anything get done? How would I find answers to any questions? What would this mean? What in the world was the matter with me?

"Come on in," the secretary said. "Have a seat and he will be right with you." The neurology fellow sat down with me. The hall we had just walked down ended in a semi-circular space, and each department leader had an office there. The psychiatry department was next to the internal medicine department. I hoped that no one from next door would see me. I still couldn't read.

I remember what happened next as though it were happening today.

The secretary walks into my supervisor's office and closes the door. I wait. I feel very straggly and unkempt from the night's work, but strangely, I'm not very worried about this. About five minutes later, the door opens, and my supervisor calls me from inside, "Sarah, come on in." I walk inside the inner office and sit on the couch.

My supervisor is a kind man. I feel like laughing for some reason. The neurology resident sits across from my supervisor and explains that I called him very early this morning, unable to read. He tells him that I am the only intern on my service, and I am carrying a double patient load. He tells him that I have not had a day off in three weeks and that I haven't slept or eaten for at least two days.

My supervisor gets up and comes over to sit next to me. He asks me how I'm feeling. I say, "I can't read anything. The letters look like gibberish."

He smiles at me and pats me on the back. I don't understand why no one seems worried about this. I lean back on the couch and look out of the window at the trees sprouting new green leaves. He stands up and says, "I'll be right back," and walks out of the room.

A few minutes later, he returns with the chairman of the internal medicine department. I sit up straight. I like him, but I am wary of what might happen since I didn't show up to morning report. I feel kind of sick to my stomach. The chairman smiles at me a little sadly.

"What's going on?" he asks.

My supervisor replies, "Well, you have Sarah here, one of our interns, on your service this month."

The internal medicine chairman interrupts him and says with a smile, "I know! We are trying to steal her away from psychiatry to train in internal medicine. She is doing a great job with us!"

My supervisor then tells his colleague how much I have been working and that I am going to need some rest. I don't understand why he doesn't mention that I can't read. Also, the internal medicine chairman obviously hadn't been at morning report since he is still smiling at me. He calls his chief resident and asks him to come to our meeting. Now I really feel nauseated. My absence from morning report (especially with such a complex patient to review) could mean the end of everything. And, I think, if I can't read, I can't keep working anyway. I want to ask for a CT scan of my head, but it feels too hard to talk, so I just sit still.

Everyone makes themselves a cup of coffee. I shake my head when they offer me one. I am wide awake. Then the internal medicine chief resident walks in. He looks annoyed. He ignores me and asks his department chairman why he was paged. The chairman says quietly, "Sarah is going to take some days off. You need to arrange for coverage for her patients."

The chief resident shakes his head and says, "She is the only intern on her team, we can't do that."

"You assigned someone from psychiatry as the only intern on a team?" the chairman asks.

The chief resident nods and simply says, "She's good."

"Well, you need to figure out how to cover her patients because she will be out for a few days." He turns to me, "Sarah, can you give us your patient list?"

I reach into my white coat pocket and grab both my multiple-page list and my stack of index cards. I stand up and walk across the room, handing these all to the chief resident, who stares at them. I remind myself that since I can't read, it doesn't matter anyway.

The chief resident walks out of the room. The chairman of internal medicine stands up, walks over to me, touches my shoulder, and says, "I'm so sorry." He walks out with his coffee cup in hand.

I think, *If he is so sorry that I can't read, why isn't anyone doing anything about it?*

My supervisor comes over and sits by me again. He says to me, "Now, you are going to take three days off starting tomorrow. I want you to go home and rest and eat, and after a day or so, go for a walk and maybe go to a movie or go shopping or read a novel, whatever you want."

Staring at him, I say, "I don't think I have that much vacation. I'm saving it all for June."

"This isn't a vacation. And don't call anyone here at the hospital. We'll call you on the third day to see how you're doing."

"But I can't read!" I say, now feeling tears in my eyes. "How will I even get home?"

"By driving," he says, smiling at me again.

"How can I drive if I can't read?"

"You know the way home," he says. "I think later on today, or maybe tomorrow morning, you'll be able to read again." I sit there and stare at him. What I know is that either he is right, or I have a catastrophic brain condition. In that moment, I am too tired to worry anymore. I nod my head.

The door opens, and his secretary walks in. Her arms are full of grocery bags almost overflowing with food. She says, "Let's go, Sarah. I'll walk you to your car. This food is for you." I stand and walk out with her, looking over my shoulder at my supervisor as I leave. He waves at me.

The secretary smiles and says, "Go home and rest. And don't call anyone here. Give me your pager. We will call you in a few days."

We walk to my car in the hospital parking lot. She gives me the bags of food, and I put them in the back seat. She reaches out and hugs me and whispers, "We will see you very soon! Don't worry about anything!" and she starts back toward the hospital.

Alone in my car, I wipe my eyes and shake my head. I put the key in the ignition and turn it on, saying a tiny prayer that I can, indeed, get home. And I drive.

Thirty minutes later, I park outside my apartment in D.C., go inside and take a shower, trying not to think about anything. I crawl into my bed. Almost immediately, I fall asleep.

The next day when I woke up, I could barely remember what happened the day before. All I remembered was that I had been told to stay away from work for three days. For some reason, I trusted my memory in this. I laid in bed for a long time before I got up and slowly got dressed. I decided to walk across the street to Glover Park. It was spring, and green was everywhere. I walked for a couple of hours, brushing my fingertips over the green buds on the trees. When I began to feel sleepy, I came home, ate a sandwich, took a shower, and crawled back into bed. I tried to read a novel but couldn't stay awake.

On day two, I remembered that I had been told to go see a movie or go shopping. I drove to a suburban shopping area, one far away from the hospital. I wandered around a mall for a little while and then drove home. When I got home, I ate a little more than I had the day before, took another shower, and again went to bed.

When I woke up the third day, my telephone was ringing. I answered it. It was my supervisor checking on me. He asked me how I was feeling, and I told him I felt better. When he asked me if I could read, I said, "I am too tired to read at night. I just fall asleep."

He asked again, "But *can* you read?" I stood very still as the memory of not being able to read washed over me.

"Yes," I whispered. "I forgot that I couldn't read the other day. I can read now."

"That's great!" he said. My stomach hurt as I imagined being asked to return to work. Would they ask me to come that same day? The next day? Over the weekend? I felt my eyes tear up. I couldn't tell if I felt more anxious or ashamed or both.

He then said, " We want you to stay home until next Monday when you rotate to a new team."

"I don't have enough vacation for that!" I protested.

"Don't worry about anything," he said "Just keep resting and read something for fun. You will feel much better by next week. See you then!" And he hung up.

So I had another five days to stay home. I hadn't told any friends or any family what was happening. I picked up the novel lying on a table and opened it. Yes, I could read just fine. It all seemed like a bad dream. But I didn't go back to the hospital until the next Monday, as instructed.

I took a lot of walks in the woods over the next few days. I knew that my intern year would soon come to an end. It seemed as though I would still be a doctor, even after all this. As I felt the sun streaming on my face through the new leaves as I walked, I remembered the three blizzards of January that I had endured. I admitted to myself that I missed the sunny beaches of Galveston. I missed my community and my friends. I loved D.C., but it wasn't home. I wondered what another three years of psychiatry residency here might do to me.

For the first time all year, I acknowledged that I wanted to go home. This was the first time all year I'd had any time to even ask myself the question. I couldn't tell if this was a failure or not. I am pretty sure that I was too burned-out to care. Looking back, I can see that this was one of the first times that I paid attention to myself during my psychiatry training. Everything had almost magically stopped for a few days, and after sleeping, I woke up to myself and the wisdom of the woods. I knew in my heart that I needed to follow the sun back to Texas. I knew in my heart that I could find a way. I didn't yet know that I would fall in love, that I would do an additional residency in child psychiatry, that I would live near Galveston for the next thirty years, marry, and have a child. I only knew, in the deepest place inside me, that I wanted to go home.

Chapter 12

PRACTICING MEDICINE

First there was the call to become a healer, delivered in a dream. Then came four years of medical school on Galveston Island. Residency training followed, with an intern year at Georgetown in Washington, D.C., followed by a return to Galveston for four additional years in adult and child psychiatry training. I spent nine years total learning how to practice medicine. I borrowed money, lived in tiny apartments, and mostly gave up sleep. I stayed the course and followed my dream. And then I was ready to be a doctor.

Over the next twenty-five years, I would work at three places. My first psychiatrist job was as a faculty member at UTMB Galveston. During this time, I also became the medical director for children's services in the Galveston County public mental health system. Additionally, I visited the Rio Grande Valley monthly to provide psychiatric evaluations and consultations in a time where there were no child psychiatrists in the Valley.

After two years of working at UTMB in this first job as a psychiatrist, I accepted a faculty position at Baylor College of Medicine. For three years, I worked in this system as one of the medical directors at a Houston children's nonprofit agency, DePelchin Children's Center.

My third and final position was in Houston's public mental health system, now known as the Harris Center for Mental Health and Intellectual and Developmental Disability (IDD). I stayed here for almost twenty years, beginning as a clinical child psychiatrist and ending with a sixteen-year stint as the agency's medical director for the IDD Division. I also provided oversight for the Chief Nursing

Officer and the Compliance and Medical Records Departments. During these years, I remained on the voluntary faculties of Baylor and the University of Texas Medical School at Houston.

If it sounds like I spent a lot of time practicing administrative psychiatry, that's because it's true. However, I was a reluctant leader. I loved seeing patients, especially kids and families. I loved watching patients of all kinds begin to feel better. After being invited into administrative activities, I ultimately embraced these supervisory roles. A colleague once said to me, "You still have a lot of patients, they just all belong to one giant family called 'the staff.'"

Being a medical director is still practicing medicine. I believed that my first responsibility was to agency patients and families, followed by the staff who cared for the patients and families, followed by my own supervisor and the agency board. It was an upside-down way to lead, but it served me well. Overall, I practiced medicine for thirty-five years, and in some ways, it was nothing like I expected. I know now why it is called "practicing." I practiced leading, I practiced teaching, I practiced being a midwife to healing.

Medicine was a spiritual calling for me. It was never on my list of most-wanted professions. I had virtually no pre-med preparation as an undergraduate, and so I had to spend several years taking prerequisite courses and studying for the Medical College Admissions Test (MCAT) before even applying. I knew that medicine was both a calling and my deep desire because all of the preparation went surprisingly smoothly. I felt an internal conviction that this was my path. I didn't think about what would happen if I didn't get in. Following this desire wasn't optional for me.

Desire can be tricky like this. Sometimes we say no to our deepest desire, not just because we are afraid it won't work out, but maybe because we are afraid that it will. As a young adult, I struggled to acknowledge my deep desires. I was afraid of being overwhelmed by either outcome, failure or success. The difference with saying yes to the call to become a healer was that I knew this was my next right step. I knew because of a powerful dream. I knew because of support from two spiritual directors. I knew because I was enlivened by this call.

Becoming a doctor changed not just my work, but who I was—who I am. Endless amounts of information and the privilege of witnessing healing made a heady concoction that satisfied me for years. I learned that saying yes to the deepest desires does not disappoint. Life is never the same again. We are never the same again.

Practicing medicine became my introduction to mystery. Medicine is a profession where patients want answers. The truth is that almost always the answer to any question is that we can't know for sure. Wearing a white coat signals authority, expertise, cleanliness, and "being right." We want to trust our doctors. But trusting a doctor isn't the same as the doctor being right every time. No one is right every time. In even the simplest situations, surprises both welcome and unwelcome can and do arise. We are taught to do things right, to think consistently, and to make reasoned and reasonable decisions. I wanted so badly for each outcome to be a good one. I wanted to know the answer, to help relieve suffering, to witness miracles. All of this happened over and over again, but not because I was right every time, or even most times.

As an administrator, I encountered conflicts of all kinds. Most of the time, I didn't automatically know the next right step. Most of the time, I had to learn to wait, to be quiet and listen, to discern as best I could what to say and what to do. To first do no harm, and then, if harm was inevitable, to work to do the least harm possible. This meant I had to accept the mystery of not knowing over and over again. Practicing medicine with integrity means being honest. Honest about not knowing as well as about knowing. The archetype of the healer becomes an expectation and a projection. But the only way to practice medicine as a response to a call and a deepest desire is to ultimately accept the mystery. To respect the ambiguity that is human life. To tell the truth and be humble enough to say, "I don't know, I'm not sure."

There were many times that it seemed practicing medicine stretched me between the desire to be a healer and the frustration of the mystery of not knowing. There were times I felt like I might break in two. I never wanted to give up, but I often felt anxiety and pain related to lack of control. It was here, as in other contexts, that

63

belonging became my salvation. Practicing medicine can be isolating. It can be exhausting. The pressures are intense, and the responsibility can feel overwhelming. The advent of new technology and new pharmacology has led to better outcomes for many patients. The same advances have changed the practice of medicine and in theory made seeing more patients possible. But these advances didn't take into account the healing component of the patients' relationships with their doctors. I fought against attempts to demand that psychiatrists' time with patients be shortened, and I advocated for longer visits. This was an unpopular stance from a financial perspective, and for good reason. Reimbursement rates for psychiatry are routinely low and misrepresentative of the cost of the service. Nonetheless, I could never turn away from the eyes of our doctors pleading for more time with patients, with families, with their own need to learn more. Again, belonging ruled the day. I felt strongest when I reached out to fellow medical directors for support. Psychiatry is a lonely practice, but community and belonging brought closeness and empathic understanding. I held space for my colleagues as they did for me. We shared tears and triumphs. My doctor friends knew and understood the incompatibility of offering healing and not always being right. We found ourselves side by side in the middle of the field. I will never be able to adequately thank those physicians who taught me, who worked beside me, who cared for me and allowed me to care for them. Together, we were able to do what alone seemed impossible.

What did I love most about practicing medicine? The intimacy of being a part of people's lives during important moments and the desire to support healing. The invitation to never stop growing, as a physician and as a person.

What challenged me the most? The inability to practice perfectly, whether in the clinic or in the boardroom, and the burden of not knowing answers when others expected them. The anxiety and exhaustion of the pressure to always be present.

What was I most thankful for? The companionship of belonging and the bedrock foundation of community. The colleagues who were tireless and never gave up. That, together, we discerned what was right in the moment and that we stood together on behalf of our patients.

There is a story I have told many residents and medical students. When I was a third-year medical student on a clinical rotation, one student on our team seemed to always be right. The rest of us came to the hospital very early, looked up patients' lab results, wrote them on index cards, and were disheveled by the time rounds started. We wanted to be prepared, and we exhausted ourselves trying. The other student showed up well-rested and well-groomed just as rounds began, had no index cards, and blithely recited all the patients' lab results from memory. It was discouraging to compete with what appeared to be genius.

One day, our resident told us all to wait in a conference room while he talked with the other student, the one who recited everything from memory. He came back to us about ten minutes later. He looked in our eyes and told us that our fellow student would not be returning to the rotation. The student had been fabricating all the lab results. Our resident said, "You know, you can get away with not telling the truth in some jobs. But if you are going to lie, you need to go work in a bank or something. If you are going to be a doctor, there will come a time when someone's life is going to depend on your ability to tell the truth." He told us to be the ones who can tell the truth.

Practicing medicine has taught me many things. I did my best to tell the truth whenever I could. I didn't always get everything right, and I made many mistakes. I am still a doctor. I still feel the deep desire to nurture healing in those around me and in our world. I still find that my efforts are impeded by the barriers of mystery, of not knowing, of a world that wants perfection based on quantifiable data. My efforts are impeded, but they are not extinguished. Belonging is the bridge from desire to mystery and back again. I know that I need community, as a physician and as a human being. I will practice medicine all my life in one way or another. The gift of my calling sustains me, and I pray that it helps bring light to others. Mystery will always be present, and I am thankful for the education it offers. I pray that I always remember the sacrament of belonging and the efficacy of community.

Desire, Mystery, and Belonging

May we listen to our deep desires with the reverence that they ask of us. May we be patient with the mysteries and devoted to finding the understanding that moves us forward. May we know in our bones that we do not walk alone. That we belong to each other in the middle of the night as we do in the bright daylight. That this belonging will always be our way home. May we all practice healing together as human beings in our beautiful and aching world.

FAMILY

Chapter 13

FAMILY

We all have families—families we are born into, families we choose. There are the families we grow up in and the families we grow ourselves. We learn much about life from our family experiences. If we are lucky, we know joy and love. Not everyone is lucky. Our earliest traumas occur in the arms of family. And even in the absence of overt trauma, we know pain. From the simplest pain of a lost teddy bear to the unimaginable loss of a parent's death, we know pain, and we learn what happens next: how to heal, and if not to heal, how to not hurt anyone else. We learn desire, mystery, and belonging for the first time from those who care for us as children. And for the rest of our lives, we continue to explore and experience desire, mystery, and belonging as we grow into creating our own families—biological families and families of choice.

The first story, **Katie**, is about our daughter. It is about the journey to having a child. There were twists and turns, and even though I am a physician and had delivered other women's babies myself, there were new experiences every step of the way. Becoming a mother is a moment like no other. Life changes forever in that moment. The desire for a child burned in me for a long time, but it would be years before I would know this joy. Those years were filled with mystery and the call to faith. It was belonging in marriage with my husband that held me strong, that kept my faith alive. This is only the beginning of Katie's story. It has been a glorious ride for us.

Time Travel, the second story, brings me back to the town I grew up in: Longview, Texas. Katie spent her first year of teaching at a high school in a nearby town, and she lived in Longview. Helping her move in, I made a trip to east Texas and stayed for a week, much longer than I had spent there in many years. Both of my parents had died some years before, and we had buried them in a lovely rural cemetery just north of Longview. That week, I was visited by the friendly ghosts of my childhood as well as the blessing of friends still living, both my friends and my parents' friends. Again, the movements of desire, mystery, and belonging danced together that week.

The last story is **Tallahassee**. I traveled with my sister to Florida one late summer to say goodbye to our last remaining aunt, the last relative from the generation before us. We were able to visit with her a couple of times, and we stayed for a few days, spending hours talking with our cousins, some of whom also traveled to visit. The experience of saying goodbye sadly comes to every family. We also found the treasure of re-connection, of shared Christmases and summers as children, of learning to know each other as adults with our own families.

Families are born of desire. From the moment we say yes to our family, the years bring mystery after mystery, and we travel together in the ambiguity of life that we all know well. Belonging in family may be our greatest strength, and when it is not, we can create new families and new strengths. It is here that we learn who we are. It is here that we find the courage to move forward as a human family.

Chapter 14

KATIE

I write this sitting in Galveston, looking out at the Gulf of Mexico. Today is my daughter's twenty-second birthday. She is backpacking through Europe with friends and will be home next week. I remember so many birthdays with Katie.

- The first one, when I took the day off from work and took her to Sears for photographs.
- The one at the skating rink.
- The one at the bowling alley.
- The ones with sleepovers.
- All the ones when some of her friends would be out of town on vacation because she was born in the middle of the summer.
- Her thirteenth, when she was in Ohio visiting her grandparents.
- Her fifteenth, when I took her and her friends to dinner at a restaurant and everyone ordered pancakes.
- Her sixteenth, when I was away at a conference and Bob took her to get her driver's license and she passed the driving test.
- Her twenty-first, when she was in Costa Rica studying abroad where the drinking age is not twenty-one but eighteen.
- This one, when she is backpacking through Europe with friends and has been a legal adult for a whole year.

Giving birth was such a miracle in my life. Bob and I were open to having children, but we were not at all sure that it would happen, given our "older" ages. I was thirty-eight and he was forty-four when we got married. After a couple of years of marriage, we felt ready. I yearned deep in my body to have a baby. My gynecologist cheerfully advised me to just forget contraception and see what happened. I was traveling for my job each month, and it seemed that the weeks I was traveling somehow coincided with the days I was ovulating. Within three months, however, I became pregnant.

We were very excited. I bought a little bib that said "Daddy Loves Me." We talked about names: Elizabeth for a girl, and Zachary for a boy. However, our excitement would not last for long. At eight weeks into the pregnancy, I went to the bathroom on a Saturday and saw that I was spotting blood in my underwear. I tried to call my doctor, but she was out of town. I called the covering doctor and was advised to stay in bed and rest. I was told that the bleeding might stop or that it might continue, and I would feel cramps and perhaps experience loss of tissue along with the bleeding. I was told that the emergency room could not help me and that the best thing to do was to stay home in bed and call my own doctor on Monday.

All that weekend, I stayed in bed. The bleeding did not stop. I felt dazed. I saved all the tissue that passed through me. Sadness moved into our bed and stayed for the whole weekend.

On Monday, I called my doctor. When we went to see her, she examined me and told us that I had suffered a miscarriage. I gave her the tissue fragments I had saved in little plastic containers. I was thankful that sometime in the middle of the night, I had gotten up and silently baptized the tissue while praying the words "I baptize you in the name of the Father and of the Son and of the Holy Spirit" in my heart. As she continued her examination, I felt dizzy and closed my eyes. I went back home, not pregnant anymore. My hormones exploded within a few hours, and I stayed home from work for a week, crying much of the time. I realized that I had never understood how painful miscarriage can be. I remembered being a young girl and my mother telling me that my aunt had "lost a baby" and wondering where the baby went. I knew now that I would try to never again minimize it or to look the other way, but instead I would do what I could to offer support to anyone experiencing pregnancy loss.

My doctor advised us to wait three months before trying again. I was afraid that we had lost our only chance, but four months later, I was pregnant again. This time, I prayed every day. I was nervous each time I went to the bathroom for nine months. But, despite my anxiety, I loved being pregnant. I knew now what a miracle it was. I talked to my baby all the way to work and back. I was militant in my refusal of any invasive procedure but later agreed to amniocentesis so that I would have, in the words of my gynecologist, a "peaceful pregnancy." I was sleepier than I had ever been in my life. As the pregnancy progressed uneventfully, we began to "nest" and prepare. We would lie in bed at night practicing for the delivery by breathing together. We bought a crib made of the same wood as our bed. We found out that our baby was a girl, and we agreed on three girls' first and middle names. We went to childbirth classes at the hospital, and Bob won the dad's diapering race.

I stopped work on July 1st, four days before my due date of July 5th. Maybe we would have an Independence Day baby! We were ready, but the baby wasn't. I went to the doctor on July 6th, hoping that my back and hip pain might be signs of labor. She examined me and said they weren't but that the baby was ready to be delivered. Then, she stood still and looked at my face. She asked what we would think about medication to help induce labor the next Saturday.

We said yes, yes, yes!

When first becoming pregnant, I made a birth plan for natural childbirth with no induction and no anesthesia. I now understood that trusting my doctor would allow me to relax into the flow of what was to come. I knew that childbirth would not be easy, but I felt the call before I had even seen Katie. I needed to trust in the unknown— in the mystery. This desire of mine, for this amazing, wonderful child, could only be realized by my consenting to the mystery and embracing the support of belonging with those around me.

And so, very early in the morning on July 8th, Bob and I went to the hospital. We settled into a labor room for what would be an eighteen hour labor. He ate pizza and Girl Scout cookies, and I ate ice chips. At the beginning of my labor, I refused all anesthesia. After six hours, when the contractions induced by the medication started to feel like a truck driving through my body, I agreed to a small dose of something in my IV. I noticed the slight burning as the medicine was pushed in, but no change at all in the contractions. I said to forget any more of that stuff.

Several hours later, I felt as though a whole freight train was driving through my body. Between friends coming in and out of the delivery room, I closed my eyes and did my best to breathe. I was hungry and thirsty, asking again and again for ice chips. Periodically, we would hear loud noises from nearby rooms. Sometimes they sounded like screams. Our pediatrician arrived and announced that she was taking her four small children to see the Lion King movie, and she would be back later. I figured this might mean things could take a while longer. My nurse whispered to me, "You know, the anesthesiologist on call is down the hall drinking coffee. This might be a good time to consider an epidural."

I looked at her, remembering that my sister had also planned for no anesthesia during her first pregnancy and late in labor changed her mind, saying to her nurse, "You mean I could be numb from my chest down?" At that point, I also agreed to an epidural and soon felt the odd relief of numbness flowing through me after ten hours of induced contractions.

A few hours later, it was evening and my doctor arrived, examined me, and said, "Okay, I think you can push now." I looked at my husband and scrambled into a pushing position. I pushed and pushed. I pushed for almost an hour.

When the baby's heart rate slowed down momentarily, my doctor said she thought we should deliver the baby via cesarean section. I looked in her eyes and said, "Let's go." I had wanted no induction, no anesthesia, and no C-section. But now, all I wanted was a safe delivery of a healthy baby. My only worry was whether I would really be numb, but again, I said yes to trusting the anesthesiologist. It is not always easy for a doctor to trust other doctors, but I said yes again and again that night. A few minutes later, I was wheeled to an operating room.

The pediatrician was there, gowned and gloved, along with my doctor, my nurse, and my husband. She said her kids loved the movie.

My doctor said, "You may feel a little tugging." And in only a few minutes, just like that, I heard Katie's cry. She was on my chest within a moment.

Bob and I looked at each other and said, "She is Kateri Ann," as together we chose her name. I cried a little along with my baby. We held her there on my chest while my doctor sewed my incision together.

The next few days, we three stayed together in the hospital. There were lots of miracles. She breastfed easily and eagerly. As she slept on Bob's chest, I stood up to shower successfully without my incision popping open like I thought it might—like it felt like it would. When we were being discharged, my doctor said, "We'll see you back next year when you decide to try for a son!"

I realized then that this birth, after all, was gloriously ordinary. This desire, this mystery, this belonging, this call, is among the most intimate and tender parts of being human. We would soon learn that we were so thankful for our happy, healthy baby that for us, the right thing was to live gratefully with one child. But I loved that my doctor saw that I could have another one, that it was okay to say that out loud. Because I still also carry in my heart the one I lost. And the one I gave birth to, and her friends, and my nieces and nephews of what are now two generations.

Because this call, this desire, and this mystery, this is how the human race continues. It's the most ordinary thing. We all arrive in life the same way, and yet it is the most miraculous thing. Each of us is growing into our own DNA and our own family and our own soul. We live in the promise of the greatest love of all—the love of the Holy One, who is faithful and true.

Happy Birthday, my beloved daughter. Happy Birthday to us all, everyone.

Chapter 15

Time Travel

Five days ago, I put Scout, our 100 lb golden retriever, in my car and set off on the four-hour drive to Longview, Texas. Our daughter Katie had moved to Longview the day before for a nearby teaching job. Scout is actually her dog, and for the first time since her high school graduation, she is living in a place where he can be with her.

Scout likes riding in the car, but I wasn't sure if he could tolerate a four-hour drive. I also wasn't sure I could manage him if he couldn't because he is stronger than I am. I wasn't sure he would go up or down the steps to reach Katie's third floor apartment. But in spite of my concerns, all that mattered, really, was getting him to Katie. For the record, Scout has done great in his new digs.

This story is about expectations and how I can be surprised, by myself and by those around me. It is about the clear value of not making assumptions. Maybe it is about finally growing up and seeing the dance of desire, mystery, and belonging blend into grace in real time.

I moved to Longview at the age of five and graduated from high school there. It is a town of about 80,000 people in the piney woods of east Texas, near lakes and rolling hills. When I was a kid here, there were only 40,000 people. A lot has changed, but much remains the same.

Although I'd long since moved away, both of my parents lived in Longview until my father died in 2004. He was sick for some years before that, and homebound on hospice care. Beginning in the mid-1990's, I made the four-hour road trip from the Houston area to Longview about every other weekend. In those days, I was the designated family healthcare advocate, and both of my parents had ongoing health needs. I would buckle baby Katie into her car seat and hit the road after work on Fridays. Our family relationships have generally been very close and loving, and this belonging carried me through the stress of those years most of the time. After my father died, my mother moved to our town to be near us in an assisted living facility. She lived another four years before dying in 2008. It is safe to say that my associations with Longview during those years were nervous, tiring, and sometimes painful. There wasn't much talk about caregiver fatigue in those days, but I was a poster child for this experience. My sister moved to our town after a few years, and we shared the responsibility of caring for our mother; my other two sisters came when they could from distant states. It took a village, and thankfully, we had one.

Since my mother died, my travels to Longview have been few. I made a couple of trips to settle estate business and roughly annual trips to visit the cemetery. While there, I generally hid out and read in my hotel room.

At eighteen, I had been more than ready to move away. As a shy introvert, my high school claim to fame was mostly academic. I'd had close friends, but they'd all scattered to college like I had. I fell in love with Austin and decided my goal would be to become a lifelong Austinite. This didn't happen, as I later became attached to the Houston-Galveston area, which was a better fit in the long run. Regardless, I knew I wouldn't live in Longview again.

Imagine then my surprise when our daughter, after her own graduation from college, said she was going to teach in east Texas and live in Longview. Even more, I was surprised when, after moving into her apartment on a Friday, she attended my parents' longtime church two days later on Sunday. I grew up attending this church; in fact, my parents and I were charter members. It was and is a progressive Presbyterian church. Katie reported that she was swarmed with love from friends of my parents as word got out that she was at the service. Quite the contrast to my own seclusion in a hotel room. Katie also made a coffee date with the church's co-pastor and signed us up (because I was coming to bring the dog) for the weekly Wednesday night supper.

This was my first inkling that maybe my adolescent assumptions might have been a little shaky. I live with the recurrent conviction that our children are our greatest teachers. I would soon learn this yet again.

The day after I arrived, Katie went to a local coffee shop in downtown Longview for her coffee date with her pastor.—the same coffee shop in which I am writing this story two days later. Katie's pastor works in this coffee shop on Tuesdays. She is not a barista. She remotely works her pastor job here.

That night, we went across the street from the coffee shop to an event at the local microbrewery. When I was growing up, Longview was in a dry county. Almost no one drank, and if they did, they had to travel to the county line to buy alcohol. This event was called "Theology on Tap," and the topic was immigration. There was an excellent panel presentation and nine local churches had clergy present. One hundred and twenty people were in the brewery, drinking beer and listening and talking. I was sensitized to the topic at hand due to my personal involvement in Houston. I was surprised to hear all three panel speakers speak to a pro-immigration stance as a Gospel imperative. The table next to us was overflowing with members of my childhood church, drinking beer and water and applauding the speakers. Looking around, I saw many small groups sharing support for immigration and for social justice. I did not expect this from the town where I grew up.

My first epiphany was that time had not stood still when I left Longview. That perhaps in my own liberal point of view, maybe I had really underestimated this community. I had been stuck in my own assumptions for many years. I was very happy to sit at a table with a good beer and listen and talk with those at our table about how stories of the immigration crisis and separated minors have touched us and how we might help.

The next night, we went to the church for the traditional Wednesday night family supper. As we walked in the familiar doors,

I felt like I was eleven years old again, the age at which I had first crossed this threshold. I pointed out a quilt square hanging in the hall that my mother had made in 1990. My name and my parents' names were listed on a plaque by the front door along with the other charter members. I belonged here in some real sense, though I had not been inside since my mother's funeral ten years ago.

We walked into the large room where dinner was served. I found high school friends registering diners. Soon, I was face to face with many of my parents' closest friends. While they mostly must have been in their 80s and 90s, to me they still looked young. Their faces were glowing as they said hello, reached out to hug me, smiled, and in a few cases, became teary. I felt only kindness despite the length of time I had been away. The "new" pastors were also very friendly (though not really new anymore). Katie seemed very much at ease, moving through the conversations with my mother's social grace. It was a moment indifferent to time and space. My mother and father, their friends, my daughter, and myself were all present in this room, in spirit and/or in flesh. Time melted away, and I let go. Let go into the love of these good people and the love of my parents and sisters and husband and daughter. Love as strong as death, as the Song of Solomon says (8:6). It hardly seemed real, this moment in time. I knew deep inside that my invitation here was to just let it be. To breathe and to let it be.

My second epiphany parted the veil of mystery for me in a very concrete way. My desire in coming to Longview was to bring Katie her dog, to help her settle into her apartment, and then to slip back home after a few days. I am still going home in a couple of days, but I have been touched with the realization of how much I didn't know about Longview. The truth is that my usual introverted hotel hiding was self-protective—not just from the sadness of missing my parents, but from the joy of their lives that still beats in the hearts of their dear friends. It was their belonging, their life in community, that has survived with great joy the death of their physical bodies. It is their dear friends who now ease my heart, and I know that these friends, both new and old, will be available to Katie should she need them.

And they are still available to me and my sisters. The desire of this church to further social justice over many years and the mystery of my own fixed assumptions were united in the practice of belonging, the practice and strength of community. For my parents' generation, for my generation in our own way, and now for Katie's generation, in whatever iteration is created and comes next.

Tonight, we are having dinner with one of my best friends from high school who still lives in Longview. I reached out to initiate our meeting because I want Katie to meet her. I was her bridesmaid. We were on the swim team together (she swam, I was the manager). Her daughter is visiting her, and we will all meet for dinner at a restaurant my father loved. Time traveling once again. What a blessing to gingerly and oh-so-slowly meet redemption on the streets of my own hometown.

May we never fear our deepest desires, and may we honor them in whatever season they arise. May we remember to practice reverence within our mysteries, as for all we know, time is truly our friend and not our enemy. And may our willingness to belong, to set our own assumptions aside and open our hearts and minds to discerning community, inform our decisions, guide our values, and bring us home to those we love and to ourselves.

Chapter 16

TALLAHASSEE

When I hear the word "Tallahassee," my mind fills immediately with images of tall, graceful trees with widespread limbs, dripping with soft and gauzy Spanish moss. Sunlight peeks through the moss and lands on my face, and warms it. I think of it as perhaps more Southern than "the South," though I'm not sure what I mean by that. The soft aroma of magnolia reminds me of an old family custom of draping loved ones' caskets with magnolia leaves. And of the nearness of those we miss who have already died.

I don't remember all of the events leading up to our trip to Tallahassee. I had spent three weeks of this late summer season in three different places: at a continuing education seminar in New Mexico, in east Texas helping my daughter settle in a new apartment and a new job, and on a Gulf Coast beach, watching waves and reading novels. I was anticipating that the next week would be spent regrouping at home, returning to routine.

Instead, on Monday evening, I waited to board a plane from Houston to Knoxville with a ticket purchased only a few hours earlier. I was flying to meet my sister in Tennessee and driving ten hours the next day to Tallahassee. Our aunt, our last living relative from our parents' generation, had entered residential hospice care, and we wanted to see her. She had lived in Tallahassee for many years.

I didn't just want to see her. I had a deep desire to see her. The kind of desire I am learning to pay attention to. The kind of desire this book is about. I am the oldest of the cousins, and I wanted—needed—to reach out to my aunt. I needed to see her and whisper to her and touch her hand. I needed this connection, this bridge, from her generation to mine. I longed to be in this liminal space beside her for a few moments.

As we drove into Tallahassee, the soft Spanish moss waved from the sturdy and abundant old trees. The late afternoon was hot and steamy. The hospice building where my aunt was staying was welcoming and quiet. We saw her for a brief visit and touched and breathed in the mystery of this tender exchange. There was a beautiful light in the room, diffused softly on her face and hands. We shared both hello and goodbye in those moments, as well as thank you, and I love you. These are some of the words I shared, and there were others that escape me now. I kissed her and held her hands. I was filled with gratitude for this time together.

Soon after, sitting in the hospice common living area, we saw our cousins for the first time in over ten years. Although we are all well into adulthood now, I hold the powerful memory of all of us as children, visiting in the summers, playing as our parents talked and laughed for hours into the night. I sensed a connection with them that seemed to stretch beyond the years and yet was simple and natural at the same time. I was so happy to see them. Our thought had been to see our aunt and then perhaps drive back to Tennessee the next day so as not to "be in the way." As it turned out, I would remain in Tallahassee for three more days—until, through, and following my aunt's passing the next day.

The next morning, I walked around the backyard of my aunt's home. There was the swimming pool I remembered feeling so good in the summer heat, the gate to the front yard that I imagined opening the one Christmas we spent in Tallahassee many years ago, with the boys racing go-karts in circles around the house for hours. There were trees covered in soft, beautiful moss and flowers and bushes and small statues of angels. My sister and I were taking pictures when we suddenly saw a butterfly alight on a bush near where we were standing. She lifted her camera and I lifted my phone. This butterfly sat still, opening and closing its wings slowly for a long moment, like it was posing for us. I shot a quick video of those beautiful orange wings opening and closing, opening and closing. My sister and I looked at each other, and we knew this was a visitor from beyond. A beautiful messenger of new life.

That afternoon, all of our Tallahassee cousins and a couple of other cousins who had flown in that morning from Atlanta sat together in my aunt's family room. This familiar room was filled to overflowing with books, photographs, artwork and needle work, and comfortable seating. One wall was lined with books, the opposite wall had a fireplace, and the other two walls were windows to the front and back yards. It was a cozy yet spacious room in a beautiful home. We sat together and talked and laughed, as our parents had done in this room for many years. Late in the afternoon, my cousins were called to come to the hospice center, and my aunt died within the next hour.

We stayed in Tallahassee that night and the next. There was comfort to be found in being together. We ordered pizza and broke bread together, one cousin praying before we ate. We sat and talked about many things. There were memories to share as well as the much more recent experiences of our own parents' deaths and how to move forward with what came next. It seemed crazy to me that I had planned to turn around and leave earlier in the week. We stayed and made decisions just one day at a time. College students were moving into Florida State University, so most hotels were filled with parents. We changed hotels almost every night just to find a room.

But each evening found us back in that family room. Back to the desire to be together as extended family. Back to the mystery of everything from shared genetics to our parents' childhood stories to the butterfly visit in the backyard. And my last evening in Tallahassee, sitting with my sister and my cousins, I palpably felt the connection we share. The belonging that supports who we had been and who we had become. I don't have words to describe the sense of belonging we knew together as small children and now as aging adults. No family is perfect, and all families have struggles. We know that we are no different.

My aunt had died. My sister's husband came on the day I left to go home. The funeral was the next day. I am told the service was beautiful, and I know that it was. What I sense now, a thousand miles away and several days later, is my forever connection to my cousins. I feel that no matter the time or distance, we are gathered together and held by that luminous, gauzy, soft moss that floats in the trees of Tallahassee. I am ready to move forward as the oldest of my generation, doing what I can to honor who we are, our differences as well as what we hold in common. I give thanks for the desire that brought me to Tallahassee, the desire to say yes to this mystery of the unknown future and to this tender and powerful belonging.

May we trust the desire for family and for love. May we find the energy and the eagerness to swim in the mystery regardless of the outcome. May we honor belonging in all its faces, and may we know the Holy among us and those we love, every step and every moment of every day of our lives.

GRACE

Chapter 17

GRACE

Grace stands in the middle of this book. I believe that the dance of desire, mystery, and belonging leads to grace. Grace, an endangered quality in our world. Grace can be defined as "simple elegance," "courteous goodwill," or "unmerited favor." I think of it as the goodness that flows through human life, that lifts us beyond the realms of baseness and preoccupation with ourselves. Grace in our world is a sign to me of the Holy that lies around and within and beyond our experience. A sign that something greater than ourselves exists. Although we are not able to touch its essence directly, that faith can draw us close to its warming fire. Grace is goodness and giftedness we have not earned, but receive as blessing. Grace is freely given from the hands of a loving God.

The first story is **Soraya's Baptism**. It recalls a visit to church and a sacramental experience. I found myself surprised by grace that Sunday morning. One of the wonderful attributes of grace is that we are often surprised by its appearance. We don't always know how to respond. That Sunday morning, I was surprised and changed in an unexpected way, and this grace remains with me still. I pray that it always will.

The next story, **Little Ones**, speaks to the children who have been separated from their parents at the Mexico/United States border and are housed in shelters all over the country while their parents await asylum. This issue fell close to home when it was announced in June of 2018 that infants and children under two years of age were to be brought to Houston to be kept in a warehouse building just south of downtown. The local community responded with alarm and resistance, and the tiny children did not come. However, we learned that many older children were already being housed in Houston, indefinitely separated from their families. The presence of grace fueled Houston's response and continues to do so. Social justice is enlivened by grace, and we are energized to enter the mystery of how to change what cries out to be changed.

The final story, **Jesus**, is an attempt to share my own relationship with Jesus. This is a relational story rather than a theological one—an imperfect story that can only be told in the context of grace. A story that only makes sense in the presence of grace. My strongest desire, my most powerful mystery, and the most foundational belonging of my life. My treasure to share. Holy love and Holy grace.

I am a Christian, formed by grace. I am nurtured and challenged by social justice, community, and a relationship with the Holy and with the human family. It is grace that brings me hope for the future and peace in the present. I see miracles as a doctor, as a spiritual director, as a wife, a mom, a daughter, a sister, and a friend. May this Holy grace invite even a little light into our world this day, and may we live into hope.

Chapter 18

SORAYA'S BAPTISM

I am sitting in the next-to-last pew. By myself. I snuck in the front door of my own church, quietly slipping into the hundred-year-old building in midtown Houston. I have not been to church here in months, even though I am a member here. My Episcopal priest husband is serving as the interim rector at a church on the west side of Houston, so I have been going there on Sundays to hear him preach. But this church I sit in today, Trinity Church, is where I lead a monthly women's circle, where I facilitate a weekly writing circle, and where I practice individual spiritual direction. During the week, the church hums quietly. On Sundays, it sings and shouts with lavish abundance. I am feeling shy this Sunday morning as I sit quietly, bathed in the light of all colors streaming from the stained glass windows.

I am here because my friend's baby daughter is being baptized today. My friend who is in my women's circle, my writing circle, and who teaches yoga at our church. What I didn't realize until yesterday is that this is not the only thing happening at church today. One of our bishops is visiting today. He will baptize this baby and also confirm and receive several adults into the Episcopal church. This can mean a longer service and more formality. This day, however, it will mean something more.

My church is important to me. As a priest's wife, I have been part of many churches in our area. But Trinity is my home church. I found this community when my husband served as the priest for the homeless congregation, Lord of the Streets, that met each Sunday morning at 7:00 am at Trinity.

Trinity is over a hundred years old. It is in the middle of midtown Houston, a neighborhood in transition. The main campus of Houston Community College is a block away. The light rail stop outside of Trinity can take a passenger either to downtown Houston or in the opposite direction to the Texas Medical Center, the largest medical complex in the United States. Either trip is only a few minutes. Homeless persons, college students, and business people all walk the streets around Trinity. The large main worship space and the small intimate chapel are both beautiful places, filled with soft, clear light. I think sometimes about being buried here in the columbarium someday, in these brick walls.

The first time I ever came to church at Trinity, I was also alone. I was looking for a new church as my Episcopal priest husband had changed jobs. About halfway through the service, my eyes filled with tears. My heart softened and warmed, and I felt like I had come home. I talked later with the rector, Hannah, who welcomed me from her heart, offered me encouragement, and later became my dear friend. I joined Trinity. I found community and a place to do what I loved most: spiritual direction, retreats, women's circle, and writing. There was diversity here, occasional conflict, laughter, and deeply committed service to the homeless community and other persons in need. All in a beautiful space that holds the prayers of over a hundred years.

As the service progresses, the time for the baptism arrives. My friend and her family walk up to the front of the church. The sweet baby girl is baptized with water, anointed with oil, and carried around the church by the bishop as the choir sings, "I want to walk as a child of the light, I want to follow Jesus..." I often tear up at baptisms, and at this one, as the bishop walks by my pew holding lovely little Soraya, so close that I could reach out and touch her, my heart becomes warm and soft again.

Confirmations are next, along with "receptions" for those who have been confirmed in another tradition. The bishop invites the whole congregation to a few moments of silence to become aware of the Holy Spirit's presence. I close my eyes and, turning inward, I see the light kindled in my heart. Several adults come forward as planned and are confirmed and received. This part of the Episcopal liturgy is intentional and thoughtful. The bishop places his hands on each person's head and prays briefly.

Next, there are several more adults recognized and invited forward who had planned to reaffirm their baptismal commitment. These are persons who have previously been baptized and have either been away from church for a time or who are in some kind of spiritual transition and wish to be publicly witnessed recommitting to their beliefs. The bishop holds the hands of these people and again prays briefly.

As I sit in the next to last pew, my heart is filled with the spirit and trust and desire of these people. I feel thankful to be here today and happy that I decided to come. I have seen grace in these moments, and I am thankful. I open the bulletin again, ready for the next part of the service. Again, there is a moment of quiet, and I look up.

The bishop now says, "It is my practice at this point to take another few moments of silence to see if the Spirit is still moving among us. I invite any of you who feel moved to reaffirm your faith now to come forward if you desire. You don't need to have prepared or made arrangements. If the Spirit is speaking to you, please come forward."

One person, and then another, walks from their pews to the front. The bishop holds their hands and prays. As they walk back to their seats, he stands waiting. I have never seen this happen before. I feel my whole body burning with heat. My heart feels like it might catch on fire and explode out of my chest. I am still so in love with Jesus. One more person walks to the front. I stand up, not taking my eyes off of the bishop, and walk to the front. I don't care who sees or knows. I can feel my soul flowing through me, flowing with baby Soraya and all my sisters and brothers here. As I reach the bishop, I look up at Hannah, our rector, and she is grinning at me like it is both of our birthdays. I stand before the bishop; he holds my hands and says a brief prayer. I walk back to my seat and can hardly feel the floor beneath my feet. I am bathed in love and thankfulness.

The service goes on. I am hugged and kissed at the sign of peace. I walk up to receive communion, and Hannah beams at me as she places the wafer in my palm.

Near the end of the service, I look in the program and see my name as the person to be prayed for this week in the "ministry cycle of prayer:" "Sarah Flick and the Women's Circle." This happens perhaps once a year, but I have never before been present on that Sunday.

After church, I visit with my friends, many of whom were also moved by the service. I meet baby Soraya for the first time as she sleeps in her father's arms. I learn that Hannah's husband is flying to Central America today as his mother is gravely ill, and I tell him that Bob and I will pray for her.

It is Mother's Day, and all the women are offered white flowers as we leave. I thank the bishop for his presence and for his invitation. I tell him I am Bob Flick's wife, and he asks me to tell my husband that he says hello. They know each other as priests. I drive home in wonder at my unlikely, atypical, spontaneous vulnerability. I give thanks.

I went to Trinity to see a baby's baptism. I sat alone in the back, feeling shy. Within an hour, I had reaffirmed my faith without any warning, responding simply to an invitation. I am an introvert and much happier listening than talking. It was my body and spirit that spoke today as my shyness fell away, and I once again said yes to the desire in my heart. My desire for the Holy, my desire for grace, my desire for God. I believe in a Trinitarian God, a God in three persons: God, Jesus, and the Holy Spirit. Today, I was filled by the Spirit, by surprise and without expectation, and I said yes to this invitation. Yes to desire despite the mystery of spontaneously walking into this moment, unprepared. The mystery of dropping my shyness and becoming seen in the posture of reaffirming my faith. And I know that I could do this only in the context of belonging. Belonging to God, belonging to this community, and belonging to myself. Listening and responding to the desire in my own heart. Belonging to this desire above all.

I went for Soraya's baptism, and I came home changed. Desire transforms us. It can happen any day, every day. It surprises us. I could have stayed in the pew. It would have been easier. But the grace that filled me as I said yes again to the Holy in my life continues to nurture me, to hold me, to invite me forward.

May we always treasure our deepest desire, honor the mystery that is our teacher, and cherish the belonging that supports us always, in this world and beyond.

Chapter 19

LITTLE ONES

*Downtown shelter set for migrant children; Southwest Key leases
warehouse to hold up to 240 kids, pregnant teens.*[3] A picture of a brick
warehouse surrounded by high fencing. A building near Houston's
soccer stadium, only a few blocks from Minute Maid Park where the
World Series-winning Astros play. A building in the shadow of
the interstate highway that grazes the edge of Houston's downtown.
A building very near the largest medical center in the country.

This is the headline I read on the front page of the Houston
Chronicle when I woke up a couple of days ago. The news had been
overflowing with horrible stories of children separated from their
parents at the Texas/Mexico border, children who were then placed in
shelters without loved ones. And now, I read about plans to bring the
youngest of these children, babies and toddlers, to our own city. Over
two hundred of them. To a warehouse "shelter" operated by a
nonprofit group who the government contracted to operate the other
twenty-six facilities in California, Arizona, and Texas. The little ones
were coming here, right here and right now.

Immediately, I was flooded with memories of another time when
refugees came to Houston. Hurricane Katrina hit New Orleans on
Monday, August 29, 2005. I was in New Orleans with my husband the
weekend before, and we left the city a day early to escape the storm. By

---

3 Kriel, Lomi. "Downtown shelter set for migrant children: Southwest
Key leases warehouse to hold up to 240 kids, pregnant teens." Houston
Chronicle, 16 June 2018.

Thursday night, I was in the Reliant Center in Houston, seeing patients who were evacuees from Katrina. I worked that night until past midnight. When I stepped out of the building to drive home, I looked up at Interstate 610, the loop that circles inner Houston, and I saw the headlights of buses lined up coming from the east as far as I could see.

The next weekend, I was called to help set up a mental health clinic at the downtown George R. Brown Convention Center, as the facilities at the Astrodome complex were full. I spent Labor Day weekend assembling PVC pipes, hanging shower curtains for privacy, and beginning to evaluate and treat the arriving evacuees in all those buses. We saw everyone from little children to senior citizens. Some needed medication refills. Others were in the throes of trauma response. One elderly woman asked me if I would pray with her. Another asked if we could just sit for a moment and quietly breathe together. I listened to another tell me the story of her toddler grandchild slipping from her grasp as they waited on the roof of their home for rescue, falling into the floodwater, and drowning.

This became my work for the next several weeks, from early morning until midnight. It was backbreaking physically and soul-breaking emotionally. It was also an incredible privilege to see the raw human spirit up close and personal. It was inspiring to work in community, together. Near the end of my time there, I found myself in tears and unable to speak, holding on to my colleagues who were so brave and so giving. Their dedication was palpable.

The most powerful part of all that work was family reunification. So many families were separated by this huge monster storm. There was so much dedication from the volunteers, working hard all day and night to help loved ones find each other, to reunite parents and children and sisters and brothers. People from New Orleans who had lost everything rejoiced as they found each other. When the clinic work was overwhelming, I could walk over to the family center and watch reunion after reunion. Miracle after miracle.

When the center was closed, I was left with exhaustion and a strained left hip joint. My hip healed with rest, but it was harder for my soul to heal. Working in community with the Katrina evacuees was both an incredible honor and a terrifying up-close encounter with what trauma can do to human beings. I still carry so many feelings and scars on my soul from those days.

Katrina was a natural disaster. No one chose for it to happen. Now, speeding into the present, I read that this "practice" of separating babies from parents at the border is part of the larger immigration protocol of our federal government. This practice is being deliberately chosen and enforced; thousands of children are already separated from their families in shelters across the Southwest. And the little ones are coming here to Houston.

As I realized this, early Saturday morning, something moved deep inside me. Something pushed and pulled and twisted and turned inside my spirit. That something that said, "Run run run away, as fast as you can," while also saying, "Help help help in whatever way you can." I had the sense that this too is a moment in history, a moment to be part of the human family. A moment to say yes, even as my memories of Katrina threatened to flood me all over again. A moment that reminded me of why I chose to become a child psychiatrist: to help kids. To help little ones.

I spent the weekend gathering a group of friends who also wanted to help in some way. We created an email group and committed to sharing information to discern ways we might be able to help. I contacted a friend who works with Episcopal Migration Ministries and learned that she was working with the ACLU and planning a trip to the border and/or a visit to the Houston facility and that I could be invited to join them. I contacted my Congressional representatives. I tried to pray. I felt something happening as my community reached out to each other. The movement in my soul would not let me sleep. I read and read and read—Facebook, Instagram, Twitter, the Houston Chronicle, the New York Times. I packed for an upcoming trip to Europe. I celebrated Father's Day with my husband and our daughter. I remembered my own father, who died fourteen years earlier, and I considered how completely horrified he would be by these border family separations. I sat in church and heard my husband preach about

Ezekiel, the Gospel of Mark, and about the words of Emma Lazarus on the Statue of Liberty.

Something is happening here. The worst of times and maybe—hopefully—the best of times. This movement in my soul I have come to know as desire. The deepest desire. For life and wholeness. For making a difference. For standing for the good, for carrying the light. Even in the tiniest of ways. This desire is unmistakable to me now. And, of course, it leads straight to the mystery. How did we ever, ever get to this place? And how on this good green earth will we ever get to the other side? No one knows. I can't possibly know or even imagine. This is so complex and overwhelming. These little ones strike hard at my very heart. At everyone's heart, whether it is acknowledged or not. The way forward is unknown. And, as always, to follow this desire, I must consent to this mystery. Even though I hate it.

Belonging is yet again the bridge. I would be so much more comfortable hiding inside myself. If reading alone were enough to help, I would be happy to read all day. However, isolation will never get us through the mystery to our desire. It just won't. The way forward is belonging, whether that is to just one other person or to a community of thousands. Or both.

When I learned about the little ones coming to Houston, I couldn't pretend I hadn't known it. My first instinct was to reach out. To reach out to those who I knew cared and would want to help. To create community in the midst of horror. I found friends from different places who said yes to coming together, to engaging in different ways, to sharing time and holding space and looking for the way forward, all together. I created an email group of these friends and titled it "Little Ones." These were the only words that felt right to use. It was only a beginning, but I could already see the movements of desire, mystery, and belonging cycling together. This tells me that this is a spiritual moment, a spiritual issue. That the core of who we are as humans is at stake, and the transcendence of what lies beyond us is at hand.

May we know the deep desire of wanting to care for and protect the little ones in our lives, the little ones in our world. May we have the courage and the strength to enter the mystery and consent to the unknowable. May we always remember that belonging bridges our desire and our mystery and that we do not walk this path alone, that community of any kind kindles hope and grace in our midst and in our souls.

Chapter 20

JESUS

A statue of St. Kateri Tekakwitha stands in front of the Cathedral of St. Francis in Santa Fe, New Mexico. Behind the cathedral stands a bronze statue of St. Francis of Assisi, dancing in the wind. A statue of Mary, the mother of Jesus, stands at an entrance to the Santuario de Chimayo a few miles north. Kateri and Francis and Mary. These are friends of Jesus and friends of mine. Every day, my life is infused with this light.

Our daughter is named for Kateri. My husband was a Franciscan friar for many years, and I have loved Mary my whole life. I live each day walking with friends of Jesus, friends of friends of Jesus, and on my brightest days, I remember that I walk with Jesus himself.

It is not easy to write about Jesus. I am not a theologian, so I have almost no academic vocabulary to talk about him in a professional Christian company—or in any company at all. The words are hard to find, but I want to try. I want to try because when it comes to grace, Jesus is my guy. When everything falls away, I sit with Jesus and rest right there.

As a college student, I would kneel in church, fold my arms on top of each other and the pew in front of me, and lay my head down on my right elbow. I would imagine that I was holding on to Jesus around his neck with my head on his shoulder. In this posture, I would be still and quiet. I would breathe in softly and listen for whatever words or images or thoughts might come. Reliably, I would always feel warm.

A friend told me around the time I was confirmed in the Roman Catholic church that God was incarnate, that he came to earth in human form—as a baby, not as a king—so that we would not be afraid of the Holy. And that divinity showed up as a baby so that we would know strength in weakness. Whenever I see a statue of the baby Jesus, I want to take care of it. I want to cover it up and make sure he is warm. Even more than I feel awe, I feel nurturing. The desire to love and be loved.

This is how I see Jesus Christ. The son of God, yes. The one who walked on water, yes. The one who healed, yes. And the one who I can imagine holding me as I rest in the pew. And the one who warms my heart.

I also see Jesus in the eyes of those who love me, those closest to me, and in the eyes of babies. Jesus consented to the mystery of incarnation, and in doing so, he fell in love with us. With humanity. He left us the Holy Spirit, who I believe roams the world, offering light, offering peace, offering gifts. I believe that the Spirit and the angels surround us and walk beside us.

I love Jesus. Jesus the person. He lives in my heart. God the Creator and God the Spirit speak holiness and love into our being, but it is Jesus who roamed the hills of Galilee, who was born in a stable, and who died on a cross. This Jesus speaks grace and mercy into our very hearts.

A few years ago, I traveled to Israel with my husband and daughter and a group from our church. We prepared by studying the history, theology, and geography of Israel and Palestine. What I didn't know was that the Holy Land would focus my relationship with Jesus in a whole new way. It was the power of the land itself that surprised me. The power of the Old City in Jerusalem and the ancient, secret cobblestone roads. The power of the water, the Dead Sea, the Jordan River, and the Sea of Galilee. But perhaps most of all: the power of light. Light especially in the holy places and the great light of our sun as we waited in darkness in the desert. I learned that light is everywhere, and that I was called by this land. By the desert, by the water, by the light.

The only truth I know is that light is everywhere. In the Church of the Holy Sepulcher in the Old City of Jerusalem, a holy fire burns. In this church, there is an oculus, or opening, in the top of the dome. Sunlight pours through the opening like a waterfall. Pilgrims are given slender candles lit from the holy fire. The candles smell like honey and almost melt in our hands. We carry them home.

In the Armenian cathedral of St. James in the Old City of Jerusalem, small lamps hang from the ceiling. There seem to be thousands of these tiny lamps, glowing in the darkness like all the fireflies in the world. They glow red and blue, green and golden, and they sway as the monks process by in long black robes. They move as the monks chant. There are no windows, only hundreds of tiny, swinging, hanging lamps. We sit and pray by the light.

On the Sea of Galilee, in a wooden boat, the water is impossibly blue. Sunlight sparkles and dances on the waves. There is so much light that I feel I could walk on that water. We rock in the boat and close our eyes, faces to the sun.

The only truth I know is that light is everywhere. The desert fathers taught that we should first kindle a flame in our hearts each morning. The light that does not go out. The light we desire is warmth. Light is clarity. There is always light available, even if we think it is not enough. Unexpected light is a mystery—around us, within us, beyond us. Tiny candles, fireflies, stars, the flame in our hearts. We carry the light our whole lives, with our whole bodies. We see our way by available light, one step at a time.

Jesus is my light, my brother, my heart. I don't know how to tell you how he illuminates my days and nights. I don't know how to tell you how much I love him and how much that makes me who I am. I can only say that for me, grace comes from the yes that he said. The yes that he calls me to say. I was called by my brother Jesus across the ages as I walked the hills and water's edge where he himself roamed.

When I say yes to him, trusting that he has already said yes to me, then I am home. Jesus has been bastardized and used as a weapon in inexcusable rhetoric in our time. I defy and set my face against those who would use the name of Jesus to hurt, destroy, torture, and kill. I follow the Jesus who loved prostitutes. The Jesus who turned over tables in the temple when the sacred became profane. The Jesus who welcomed small children, all of them, every one. The Jesus who said, "Don't worry." The Jesus who told us that we are the light of the world. The Jesus who I believe keeps on saying yes to loving common humanity and inviting me to the party.

I do my best to say yes, as did Mary and Francis and Kateri. My common humanity is bathed in light when I remember and when I love. For me, desire, mystery, and belonging all come home in Jesus. And this, my friends, is pure grace.

May I take one step at a time each day, breathing in love as I remember the words of the spiritual that I learned to sing in second grade, "Lord, I want to be like Jesus in my heart, in my heart. Lord, I want to be like Jesus in my heart. In my heart, in my heart, Lord, I want to be like Jesus in my heart."

CREATIVITY

Chapter 21

CREATIVITY

Creativity brings beauty to our lives. The creativity of others makes our world brighter and happier. I love to see classic works of art, and I love to visit the Museum of Fine Arts in Houston. I believe that creativity is an essential energy for each of us and that we all make art in our own way. As humans, we have an inborn desire to "make stuff" and to create. We might remember craft projects from summer camp, or maybe as adults we find knitting to be a soothing and sustaining pastime. As always, we can't anticipate the outcome of following desire, and so to create is to engage with mystery. And I have found that creating is best done in community—in some context of belonging—even if infrequent or distant. Creativity enriches our lives and reminds us of original beauty and original joy.

Becoming a Maker is my first story. It is about my early creative efforts and finding an unlikely creative champion in my elementary school principal. It is also a story about how we learn to believe in ourselves as we create. Children love to create, and we learn in our families and with our friends. The mystery delights kids who love to be surprised by the outcomes of their art. We can learn to love this surprise all our lives.

Retreating tells of some of my retreat adventures. I love the retreat archetype of leaving our everyday lives to enter liminal space. Retreats have helped me heal, have helped me find peace, have helped me know God, and have helped me create. I find the connection between the Holy and creativity on retreat. Desire, mystery, and belonging join me each time I retreat, and I come back to my ordinary life refilled and renewed.

Beverly is a story about my longtime friend who I have known since I was in college. We have been creating together for many years. Beverly's life is a story filled with creating in the midst of life's twists and turns and surprises, both happy and sad. She is a great blessing to me. I pray that we will enjoy our creativity together all the days of our lives.

Creativity begins with desire. As the artist works to bring this desire into their creation, they face the mystery of uncertain outcome. Belonging and community foster creativity. We have writing groups and knitting circles and art classes and galleries where we create and share in each other's presence. May we support the creativity that brings beauty to our world and joy to our lives, and may we know that we can always make new things if we attune to our desire, enter the mystery, and reach out in belonging.

Chapter 22

BECOMING A MAKER

My mother was a cross-stitcher. She embroidered pictures that hung all over our house—pictures that she gave friends for Christmas, pictures that still hang in my house today.

From scratch, my father and his brother made up a baseball game and a football game, both of which were played with playing cards and a legal pad and a couple of pens. My dad played these games for most of his seventy-six years, alone and with others. My grandmother graduated from college in the early 1900's and played piano. I had a distant cousin who made amazing cakes from scratch.

I learned to cross-stitch myself about the same time I learned to read, roughly four years old. I was given a hardcover book, *Things to Make and Do*, that still lives in our study. I made flannel board stories at Vacation Bible School. At Bluebird and Camp Fire Girl meetings, I learned how to knit and how to use newspapers to make "sit-upons" (cushions for sitting on the floor or the ground). I took art in seventh grade and made an acrylic painting of a water fountain. I took piano lessons starting in third grade and ending in seventh grade when I broke my arm.

I came from people who created, and I loved to make things of all kinds. However, the journey wasn't always smooth.

My first grade teacher was very young and, to my young eyes, not very imaginative. We were given worksheets (the ones with purple ink printed from the ditto machine) all day long. We were instructed to turn our papers over when we finished the assignments and sit quietly until everyone was done. From the beginning of the school year, I complied. I finished every assignment quickly, and so it seemed like I spent most of every school day sitting quietly and doing nothing.

One day, staring at the blank back of my completed worksheet, I looked up and around the room. Everyone else was still very busy with their worksheets, and our teacher had walked out of the room. I picked up my pencil and started writing. At home, I made up stories, drew pictures of them, and told them to my sisters. I didn't remember ever trying to write a story before. I started writing down one of my made-up stories and lost track of time. When I finished and looked up, our teacher was standing next to my desk, looking down at what I had written. I looked around. All the other students were sitting quietly, staring at the blank backs of their completed worksheets.

Our teacher picked up my paper and asked me if I knew where the principal's office was. I nodded, slowly and silently. She handed me my paper and told me to take it to his office. I looked up at her, not sure what was happening, and she pointed to the hall door. I thought I heard kids laughing as I left the classroom.

When I got to the principal's office, I had to wait for a few minutes with his secretary before she told me to go inside. I walked in, remembering from playground talk that the principal had an electric paddling machine in his office. My family was gentle and nonviolent, so I had no experience with aggressive behavior.

He sat behind a giant wooden desk and asked me to sit down. He asked me why I had been sent to his office. I handed him my paper, and he slowly read the front and then the back. I held my breath, sitting very still. Minutes passed. My feet did not touch the floor. I tried hard not to swing them back and forth.

Finally, he put down my paper. He reached under his desk and pulled out a brown paper bag. I thought it was his lunch. I watched him reach into the bag, rummage to the bottom, and pull out a package of Hostess cupcakes. Chocolate with white squiggle icing on top. He carefully opened the package and then looked up at me. He asked, "Would you like a cupcake?" I still had no idea what was happening, but I said yes. He handed me a cupcake across his desk before picking up the remaining cupcake and starting to eat it. We ate together in silence.

A few minutes later, he brushed crumbs from his hands. He looked at my face and asked, "Do you like to write stories?"

I took a deep breath, feeling as alone as I could ever remember, and I told him about the stories I made up, the pictures I drew of them, the stories I told my sisters, and the books I read.

When I stopped talking, he waited a moment. Then he folded his hands, leaned forward across his desk, gazed kindly into my eyes, and said, "Don't ever stop writing."

These are the words I remember. I don't remember anything else that he might have said about the story I had written down. I am not even sure I remember the story.

Then he asked, "Okay?"

I looked directly in his eyes and said, "Okay."

He stood up, handed me back my paper, and walked me all the way out of his office, down the hall, and back to the classroom. We walked into the room and I sat down at my desk. The other students all looked at him, as did our teacher. He smiled as he turned and walked out of the classroom.

This elementary school principal was my first creative champion outside of my family. He was the first person to encourage me. He knew what I didn't know then—and what my teacher didn't know— that creating is the spark of life itself, that creating can help us celebrate in good times and can save us in bad times.

There is something important about making things, whether that is writing or knitting, collaging or making music. I have the desire to "make stuff," to create for the sake of creating, to see what comes out. This desire is like a light inside me. Any time I follow this desire, I immediately encounter twinned mystery: Is it good? Am I doing this right? What does everyone think? And this makes me fear judgment, this makes me want to hide what I am making.

I can hide, or I can share. I was at a retreat once with singer-song-writer Carrie Newcomer. The group was composing a song by creating individual phrases and singing each phrase as Carrie walked around the room, touching our shoulders. I panicked. I was never going to sing by myself for Carrie Newcomer. And yet I did exactly that. I felt her hands on my shoulders, and I sang my phrase. Carrie leaned over me and said right into my ear, "You have a lovely voice!"

It is in community, in belonging, in sharing that creativity is realized. I have a lovely voice. I am a writer. I can knit and paint and sit at a potter's wheel. I am a maker, and I delight in the desire, mystery, and belonging that show up as I make stuff. We create, and we learn who we are and what life is. The circle is unbroken, and the light shines on.

Chapter 23

RETREATING

Cape Cod. Sunsets and deep woods. Glowing faces and holy laughter. Making stuff. Devotion. I recently came home from an autumn retreat in beautiful Massachusetts. If there is one practice that has helped me find and nurture creativity in my life, it is retreating. There is something about leaving my everyday time and space and arriving in nature to spend a few days listening that fills my soul every time. Time and space away from other obligations to be quiet, to create, to be together with others and alone with myself. To rest in the Holy as we find it. Retreating for me is life-giving and redeeming. It is generative. I find my desire there, I encounter mystery there, and I am surrounded with belonging there—sometimes people, sometimes spirits, most often both. Retreating is the one practice I most frequently recommend to the people who see me for spiritual direction.

Retreats have been a part of my life since I was a teenager. The archetype of retreat appeals to both the part of me that wants to "go away to a quiet place" and the part of me that wants to be in community. My earliest retreat memories were at a Presbyterian church camp in east Texas on a fall night. I was at a dance with other teenagers. I felt very shy, anxious, and ambivalent, wanting to dance and simultaneously wanting to hide. A friend a few years older came over to me and whispered something like, "You don't have to say yes, but..." and I looked up at him and we went out on the dance floor. My friend was kind, danced with me, and then asked if I wanted to go outside. The autumn night sky was overflowing with stars. I breathed deeply.

All was right with my world in that moment, and I smiled at my friend and said, "Thank you." I understood then that when we retreat, our self comes with us. And so even on a solo retreat, we are still in community. Retreats are a chance to be brave at a dance, to reach out to a friend, to watch the stars. To touch the infinite and breathe. To seek—and touch—desire.

As a college student, I became involved in what was known then as the Happening retreat. The Happening structure posed three questions to participants in small groups:

Who am I?
Who are you?
Who is God?

These retreats are still being offered to Episcopalian high school students, but when I was in college, they were offered at campus Catholic student centers. My first Happening was when I was a freshman in college and traveled to a nearby city for the weekend retreat, though I was not Catholic at the time. During the weekend, there was an opportunity for participants to "go to confession." I waited in the long line, only to tell the young priest that I was not Catholic when it was finally my turn to see him. I don't remember his words, only that he was kind and welcoming and blessed me anyway. At the end of the weekend, I found myself in tears at the sign of peace during the final weekend liturgy. I was unhappy and lonely at school but had not cried at all that year. Only while embracing as we wished each other peace did these tears of joy and relief arise in me. I fell in love with this recognition of the true peace of allowing others to see who I am and how I feel.

It was the following year, when I had transferred to a different university, that I saw another advertisement for Happening retreats. I signed up and went again, this time in a different city with a different team. Soon after, I was asked to "join the staff" and so became part of a team offering these retreats monthly to high school and college students. Our team met every Sunday evening at the home of the married couple who were the directors. These folks were surrogate parents to all of us. Their first question in any crisis was, "Have you had anything to eat?" and they would immediately produce something to eat and drink, often a peanut butter sandwich and a cold beer. They had five children of their own. On those Sunday evenings, we would sing and pray and share visions and ideas as well as work to resolve conflicts. The Happening staff became my closest community. This is where I met the person who is still my best friend.

Lifelong belonging has grown from these retreats. Recently, a reunion of Happening staff met in Dallas to celebrate fifty years of offering retreats. I learned to create community in the Happening retreats and to hold space for others. I also learned that I loved retreating and that it brought light to my imagination and spirit.

Later, I would make private journeys to local retreat centers for weekends of quiet. I would spend time reading, journaling, and lying in a hammock, looking at the sky. I would sleep and have vivid dreams. As a Jesuit volunteer, I had been encouraged to make a yearly private retreat, and it was during one of these retreats that I dreamed of being called to medical school. Often at a private retreat, I might have the opportunity to speak with a spiritual director, but otherwise, even our meals were silent. I loved the quiet. The silence made room for me, for listening to God, for wandering outside, for paying attention. I found community and belonging with myself and the Holy Spirit there.

Once married, working full-time, and having a baby, it became much more difficult to find time to retreat. When my sister invited me to a New Mexico writing retreat in 2002, my husband agreed to take care of our six-year-old daughter while I was away, and I met my sister in the Albuquerque airport. We headed for Taos in a rental car, stopping at a Walmart in Española to buy yoga mats. Looking back, I can see just how lucky we were to be able to go to the first of Jennifer Louden's Taos writing retreats. This is where I first learned yoga. This is where I was able to write an essay that helped me as I was struggling to anticipate my father's death from cancer. This is where Taos Mountain blessed me for the first of what would be many times. I met myself in Taos in nature and in community. Writing was our communion.

I would retreat with Jen a dozen times over the next sixteen years. Taos would become a home for me and a place of reverence. It is where I learned most about desire and where this book was born. I have always loved New Mexico, and now I find it sacred. Something about the enormous sky and the clear light calls to me at odd moments, and I pause and breathe, remembering again that awe and peace. Jen taught me so much about the retreat archetype, what she calls "betwixt-between time." I have learned to anticipate this liminal space and time, most especially in Taos, in the shade of the mountain where families have continuously resided in the Taos Pueblo for over a thousand years. There is magic in community and holiness in silence at these retreats, and the writing comes as grace. Jen Louden has become a beloved teacher, guide, and friend to me. I have grown very close to many of the women at her retreats. It was in Taos with Jen that I said yes to writing. I met this desire in Taos, and I learned to navigate the mystery of the unknown in writing. The belonging from Taos has become a treasure. I believe that Taos will always be a holy place for me, and I give thanks for this birthplace of my writing and, in many ways, this birthplace of myself. I give thanks to Jen for so much in my life and especially for the sacrament of Taos.

I have also had the opportunity to study at a Quaker retreat center called Pendle Hill outside of Philadelphia. One spring, I saw an advertisement that singer-songwriter Carrie Newcomer and her friend Faith Kirkham Hawkins would be offering a retreat at Pendle Hill that would include writing midrash, or retelling sacred stories. My mother had died the previous September, and I was still in the throes of recovering from both her death and the impact of Hurricane Ike in our area that year when I decided to go. The first thing I noticed when I arrived at Pendle Hill was the bright yellow forsythia bushes everywhere. The campus had giant old trees and plenty of green space and white buildings where people lived and studied, created, cooked and ate. There was a building called the "Barn" that was used for the community's daily "meeting," or unprogrammed Quaker worship. My single room was small and comfortable with a shared bath in the hall. I was on the first floor, only a few minutes' walk from the Barn and from the dining hall. Most of the food served at Pendle Hill is grown locally, and there is always a moment of silence observed prior to beginning each meal.

Our group at this retreat was small, about fifteen of us. It was amazing to be with Carrie and Faith as we retold and rewrote sacred texts in our individual contexts. Carrie would sing for us from time to time, inviting us to sing with her. We would share our writing with each other, receiving these offerings in silence. The week was very intimate and very peaceful. It was here that I began to heal more fully from that year's emotional turmoil.

Each morning, the Pendle Hill Community gathered in the Barn for "meeting." This time together was thirty minutes of what Quakers call "unprogrammed worship." We entered the Barn in silence and settled in. At times, someone would rise and simply share words that they had "received" for the group. Then the silence would continue. It was a powerful experience to begin each day by sitting in silence with a listening community. At an appointed moment, a designated member would turn to a neighbor and shake hands; this was the signal that worship had ended. There would then be an announcement and an overview of the day ahead. Guests introduced themselves upon arrival and said goodbye as they departed. I found this practice of gathering in a listening silence very grounding. This practice was fertile ground for my creativity. I readily attended meeting each morning, listening with all my heart for what might come, thankful for the peacefulness that flooded my soul as I sat in the beautiful room with sunlight flooding in, shining on the polished wood floors. Later in the day, it was wonderful to sit in the arts and crafts center and make new things. I sat at a potter's wheel for the first time there. I slept peacefully. It was hard to leave at the end of the week. As I returned home, I gave thanks for the ordinary and quiet holiness of the Quaker experience.

Finally, I have offered retreats for women myself at a local retreat center. I love the process of planning, of dreaming what words might be said, what creations might be made, what connections might be recognized. I become the one holding space for twenty other women who come to search for nature, to search for themselves, to search for God. I have felt so at home sitting in a circle with women who are retreating, who are seeking, who are resting. I believe with all my heart that the Holy Spirit of all flavors specializes in retreats. We sometimes have to go away to hear the quiet knowing. To experience the desire of who we are in our depths, where God made us. To learn to bear the mystery, the unknowing of creating and of life itself. To find belonging and community without distraction. I pray that I may continue to say yes to the invitation to be the midwife of mystery at retreats like this.

I pray as well that my own desire to retreat may always be respected and honored, by myself and by those around me. I am devoted to retreating. Retreats are the way home to my desire, to the fire inside my soul waiting to warm me. To the heart of God where all is light and all is true desire, known and satisfied. To the mystery of creating. To the belonging that sustains me.

May we always find a way to practice retreat. May we honor desire, mystery, and belonging as we make space for new life within us, for creativity, and always, for the love that waits in liminal space.

Chapter 24

BEVERLY

In the land of creativity, we find painting and watercolors and ceramics. We find poetry, novels, and weaving. We find music and movies and one act plays. We also find friends. If we are really lucky, we find friends who are creative, who come along for the whole journey of desire, mystery, and belonging. I have been gifted with many such friends, one of whom is the sister of my heart. Her name is Beverly, or as she is sometimes called, "Bevy."

I met Beverly in Austin when we were both University of Texas students. I was nineteen, about to turn twenty. We were both part of a team staffing retreats for high school and college students sponsored by the University Catholic Center, the Happening retreats. As a new staff member, I was assigned one weekend to be a support person for a small group led by Beverly. My assignment was to be an "angel" for the group leaders. She was a couple of years older and I was drawn to her spirit. Even then, there was a creative generosity that shone from her presence. She was an art major, and in those free-spirited days, I wanted to create too. I wanted to create a life that was beautiful and harmonious and peaceful. I didn't know then that Beverly and I would walk the road creating our lives together. I only knew that she was fun. And that it was easy to be myself with her.

Over the next forty years, our friendship and lives braided together. Beverly married her husband Michael when I was a senior in college. She gave birth to twin daughters the year after I graduated. Five years later, she gave birth to a son.

When their son was still a toddler, Michael became ill and was diagnosed with non-Hodgkin's lymphoma. He fought for nine years until he died, leaving my friend Beverly with fourteen-year-old twins and a ten-year-old son.

The year after Michael died, I married Bob. Beverly and her kids were the only people at our wedding who were not immediate family. But we are, in truth, family of the heart and of the spirit. When I gave birth to Katie, Beverly and her teenage son were present. Beverly became Katie's godmother.

In the years that followed, Katie was the flower girl at one of the twins' weddings. As my small family grew together, we grew side by side with Beverly and her family. I had been single while she was married, and now she was single while I was married. Our children grew up together. Most New Years Eves, we would travel to be together and raise blessing cups filled with champagne or sparkling grape juice.

Beverly moved to Houston when her children were all grown. It was soon after her arrival that she met Scott, who was my friend and colleague. Scott's wife, who I had also worked closely with, had also died from cancer. Beverly and Scott's first date happened the day after my father died. So many milestones between us, and the sweetness of our friendship as we aged was miraculous and sustaining. It was a happy day when Bob officiated at Beverly and Scott's wedding, and all of our families moved forward together.

I have been going to church with Beverly since I was nineteen years old. We have also been going to movies and art museums and on trips to other countries. Now we are both married and retired. We have navigated many rough waters, but we are strong paddlers. Our friendship itself is a treasured fruit of creativity in my life. I have learned much from her, but perhaps most of all, I have learned about creativity.

The drive to create comes from a desire deep within us. It is an ancient prompting to make things and to create beauty. Creating is, in essence, the energy of desire. It is a surrendering to the possibility of joy, even to ecstasy. To create is to yield logic to intuition, to exchange reason for magic. Over the years, Beverly has created many beautiful paintings. Some of them hang all over our house—in the family room, the living room, the hall, our bedroom, and even our bathroom. These paintings have been the backdrop of my life. They are brightly colored and filled with light. They are flowers and birds and landscapes and people. In our breakfast room, there is a painting of Mary and Elizabeth with babies Jesus and John the Baptist in their wombs.

A few years before I retired, I had a very compelling dream. I told Beverly about this dream, something we often share. The dream had to do with my struggle to let myself have what I needed in the context of caring for others. She later painted the story of my dream, a long banquet table with steaming bowls of gumbo and beaming faces all around, and it now hangs in our bedroom where I can see it when I first wake up. Her painting looks just like my dream did, even though I only told her the story and not the visual details. This is the kind of friendship that honors creativity and the desire to share each other's dreams, literal or otherwise.

Beverly has often had to fight to find time and space to paint. There have been years where kids and work and illness all kept her from the easel. Beverly has taught me that there is a cycle to creativity, and that this is both unique to each individual and impacted by life circumstances. When times are hard, it might be difficult to find time or space or energy to create, and yet creating itself can be a balm in hard times. I know when she has been painting because her face literally glows. It comes from her as easily as speech. She also makes pottery and ceramics. I will always remember Beverly guiding me the first time I sat at a potter's wheel at Pendle Hill when we attended Carrie Newcomer's retreat.

Like me, she loves to write. She holds space for my writing as I have held wall space for her art. She encourages me and writes alongside me. The truth is that we all can use a creative champion. Someone who will create beside us, encourage us, and honor our own creations.

I have learned about the desire to create from Beverly. Sharing the love of Jesus that we do, it is not surprising that we look for and find inspiration in the Holy Spirit, who we have come to know in both of our lives. The desire to create is very much kin to our deepest desire to be as much ourselves as we can. We make art from our lives, from our dreams, from our losses. These desires nestle together deep inside us like Beverly's twin girls. The desire to create can be scary, but it is far friendlier when explored with a fellow creator who knows her way around both desire and making art. Who knows her way around your life as well as her own.

Like me, my friend Beverly prefers to be in control, believing that she knows what she needs to know. The movement of mystery is a challenge for us both. Yet Beverly has surrendered to mystery over and over again in her life. She is so determined to be a worthy opponent to mystery. She will fight to win but knows how to release gracefully. She can do this, I believe, because of her faith. She has faced so much challenge and loss, but she ultimately trusted God to carry her. I have always turned to her as my mentor in this arena. She fights until she doesn't. She opens her hands and allows life to be as it is. The energy that is freed by her surrender to mystery is returned to her in her creative well. Life is mostly mystery when you look at it over forty years. Trust is hard. Yet here we are, friends for forty years despite living hundreds of miles apart for many of them. We are there for each other. Beverly encourages me to write, to make art, and when I look at her work on our walls, I do.

The final movement of belonging might seem unnecessary to explore, given our forty years of friendship. But of course, we do not just belong to each other. We have beloved husbands and cherished children. Beverly has grandchildren. We have known and loved each other's parents and said goodbye to the three who are now in heaven. We have sisters who know both of us. My daughter Katie told me not long ago that her best friend was going to be "her Beverly," and I marveled at the aspiration to be such close friends for so long. We have other friends who we are close to, separately and together. We have belonged to many church communities together. Belonging has supported us in creating a lifelong friendship that offers welcome and solace. I like to think that our laughter is a sign of hope. Desire, mystery, and belonging have set up tents in our lives, in our friendship, and in our creativity. We just keep making things, and the river of life flows on.

Today, I talked to Beverly on the phone. Previously, I had told her that I might work today cleaning out a room in our house. As we have both long lamented the crowded nature of our respective closets, she called me today to sympathize with me. Even though I wasn't cleaning the room as planned, I listened to her tell me what she was doing. She had found a box of letters from her dad, and her advice to me was to open those kinds of boxes last. She said that reading her dad's letters from years ago stopped her in her tracks, reversing time. She spent the morning in her dad's written presence. I understood. I knew and loved her sweet dad. Even now after forty years of friendship, we share these surprises. Even now, we are creating our lives and making something beautiful. The Spirit abides, and I give thanks.

May we recognize the desire to create deep within us, and may we say yes to even a tiny effort to make something beautiful. May we find good company along the way so that we can learn the ways of mystery from someone we love. May we know belonging so deeply in our souls that we are free to create, free to be who we are, free to love and be loved as children of the Holy One, painting our world in the brightest colors and in abundant hope and grace.

HEALING AND WHOLENESS

Chapter 25

HEALING AND WHOLENESS

As a physician, I am drawn to stories of healing. My experience as a healer, first as a student and later practicing medicine, was that my role grew out of my own desire to make a difference, to be a helper, and to follow the vocation of healing. I knew the desire, I accepted the mystery over many years, and I treasured the belonging I experienced in the professional medical community. I was slower to realize the role of desire, mystery, and belonging in my own health journey. These stories are about my education—not just about my own body, but also about my mind and my spirit, and about moving toward an integrated, whole sense of being.

Knowing What You Know Can Save Your Life is about an episode of cardiac arrhythmia and how my body finally got my attention in the midst of a stressful season. This event was most definitely about surrendering to the mystery of releasing control and allowing uncertainty. It was an experience that woke me up at an important time. It is a story that made me thankful.

Broken Bones catalogs a lifetime of clumsiness that led to broken bones of all varieties. I have tended to be clumsy from time to time, and even more relevantly, I am easily distracted. This has given me empathy for my patients with ADHD (attention deficit hyperactivity disorder), and it has also given me broken bones. I learned over the years to slow down and, most importantly, to pay attention. I have been fracture-free for almost ten years, and it is not lost on me that my meditation practice supports my health in this arena.

The final story is **Feeding Myself**. It tells about how, after years of dieting, often clandestinely, I found peace in intuitive eating and learning to "feast" on my own life. The diet industry profits handsomely from our insecurity, and we are exploited by a culture of fake perfection. Eating has become another way for me to care for myself and to trust my own knowing. This is a story with many layers, only a few of which can be touched on here, and it is an important story for me.

My heart, my bones, and my gut have all been involved in getting my attention and bringing me back to my desire for wholeness. They have all guided me in turning toward wholeness as I have learned to pay attention to myself and my knowing. My body, my mind, and my spirit are all in much friendlier places these days as I have learned new ways to trust and to belong to myself. My prayer is that I can help light the way for others to listen to and learn to trust themselves as whole persons—mind, body, and spirit. May we know deep in ourselves that listening to our own stories can bring healing and wholeness.

Chapter 26

KNOWING WHAT YOU KNOW
CAN SAVE YOUR LIFE

It was the spring of 2014. Things at work were very stressful. We were facing—as always, it seemed—probable budget cuts, and the staff worried about themselves and their jobs. As the division medical director, I kept reminding my staff that it was the patients that really mattered, and that we were here to serve them. All of this stress made my stomach hurt, but I told myself every day, "This is nothing new, this is just your job." I had no idea that my biggest and most consequential struggle for control lay not in my conflicts at work, but rather inside my own body. I would soon see that the path to freedom was not "out there," but rather, deep within me. It was my internal thoughts, beliefs, and obsessions that really mattered.

At 3:00 am on a Monday, as I was getting out of bed to go to the bathroom, my heart suddenly lurched in my chest as I stood up. My heartbeat took off like a wild racehorse. In the moment, I thought I could change my heart rate all by myself. I was a meditator, off and on for years and almost daily for the past several months. Surely I could change my heart rate.

I went to the bathroom. My heart kept racing.

I drank water. My heart kept racing.

I coughed and performed the Valsalva maneuver by holding my breath and trying to exhale while holding my mouth and nose closed (a procedure that sometimes slows heart rate). My heart kept racing.

I told myself, "You're not your sister" (she had a history of atrial fibrillation with rapid ventricular response and other arrhythmias, leading to multiple cardiac procedures and hospitalizations). My heart kept racing.

I meditated for ten very long minutes.

My heart kept racing.

Looking back, the truest thing I know is that I didn't want to wake up my husband—I didn't want to ask for help. And most of all, I didn't want to trust what I knew.

Finally, I reluctantly woke up Bob and asked him to drive me to the hospital. I almost drove myself, leaving him to sleep, but decided I didn't want to risk having an accident and hurting someone else.

When we walked into the empty emergency room waiting area, no one was present behind the triage desk. I walked up and leaned into the window, my heart still galloping inside my chest as I held on to the edge of the counter. A woman appeared. "Can I help you?" she asked.

I put my hand on my chest and said, "My heart is beating really, really fast and has been for almost two hours."

"Palpitations?" she asked. "Go right to room four." We came through the automatic doors, which opened with a rush of air, and walked to room four. It was a "crash room" with a lone stretcher in the middle, a huge light above, and all the lifesaving equipment I remembered from medical school lining the walls. These were the rooms where the staff rapidly assessed and treated people who may literally have been in a crash—people whose vital organs were in immediate danger. I lay down on the stretcher and two nurses appeared. Two intravenous lines were very quickly started in my arms and cardiac EKG leads were immediately attached to my chest.

A doctor ran in, looked at the monitor, and asked, "Any history of arrhythmia?"

I said, "My sister has 'a fib with RVR'" (nickname for 'atrial fibrillation with rapid ventricular response'). I wanted him to know that I knew medical terminology. What I didn't know then was why this felt important to me.

He looked in my eyes and said, "She's not the only one." I felt a very weird sense of confirmation; it almost made me happy being told there was something wrong with me after all, and I didn't make all this up.

But only almost.

I was scared.

My sister had struggled with arrhythmias repeatedly for several years. Although she was three years younger than me, I still felt way too young for this. Was this some genetic curse? Why didn't my parents have it? Ten years earlier, I had studied mind-body medicine and learned so much about the sympathetic nervous system and its response to stress. I had learned how to teach others stress management skills to rebalance the nervous system. I was meditating regularly. Was this failure of my body's ability to regulate my cardiac rhythm my fault? It felt like I needed it to be someone's fault, but whose would it be except mine?

I was scared.

I was admitted to the cardiac intensive care unit, where medication to slow my heart rate dripped into my veins for twelve hours. Eventually, my heart rate and rhythm returned to normal. All that day, I thought about caffeine and how much coffee and Diet Coke I drank. Once things finally began to calm down, I even surreptitiously drank a cup of full-leaded Starbucks (having sent my husband to the hospital cafeteria to get "real" coffee for me), while watching the monitor to see if it changed my heart rate, thinking that perhaps this was a fluke and I could return to caffeine once discharged from the hospital.

I was told to stop caffeine. I was sent home much later that day in normal sinus rhythm with outpatient cardiology follow-up. I went to see the local cardiologist who took care of my husband and my sister. His daughter had been in my daughter's class in school, and we chatted about our newly emptied nests. At his request, I wore a cardiac monitor for a week, which disclosed that I was still having small bursts of arrhythmias. He eventually prescribed a small dose of a beta blocker medication to keep my heart rate slow.

I went back to work. Everyone seemed very relieved that I had returned, but I wasn't so sure.

After some time had passed, I realized that maybe the most important question in all this was why I didn't want to wake up my husband. Why did I think I could change my heart rate and rhythm by force of will all by myself in the middle of the night? Why didn't I move more quickly when I realized my heart rate was almost 200 for over an hour?

Why didn't I want to know what I already knew? The short answer is: I hadn't yet learned that knowing what you know can save your life. I could be a doctor and a healer for anyone except for myself. I wanted to be seen as strong, more than I wanted to let myself be seen as who I was: a stressed-out psychiatrist who carried so much on her shoulders that in the middle of the night, her heart got stuck beating too fast and she couldn't slow it down.

This event would precipitate a series of questions and ultimately my spiritual inquiry about desire. I slowly came to realize that I needed to tell myself the truth.

What did this heart stuff really mean?

What did I really, truly want?

What was my real heart's desire?

Why was it so hard to allow mystery to surround me and to allow myself to surrender to the unknown?

I wouldn't know for a few more years, but this event would be an early evangelist for my next life pivot, for the invitation to release my fear of being seen as I am, and for consenting to mystery and allowing the unknown future to show up more and more in my life. It would turn out to be a critically important messenger for me. Only when I surrendered to my own knowing could a new trust in myself arise, and from there a new trust in the Holy and in life itself began to grow.

I had a strong loyalty to my profession and to my agency. I was very loyal to my family, my friends, and my church. I belonged to all those arenas. And now—not for the first time, but maybe the clearest time—I was being invited to at last belong to myself. To finally let myself really know what I knew. Now I was beginning to understand that the friendliest, most honest, and kindest reality lay in the truth deep inside me. Here at last was the beginning of healing, the origin of wholeness. Desire leading to mystery leading to belonging. It almost took my breath away. And my heartbeat became strong and regular.

Knowing what you know can save your life.

Chapter 27

BROKEN BONES

The summer after sixth grade, I was at my grandmother's home in south Georgia. It was a Sunday, and our whole family (my mother, father, three sisters, and grandmother) was in our Chevy station wagon and ready to go to church when my mother asked me if I was wearing my charm bracelet. I wasn't. A favorite local, elderly cousin had given me a charm (a little silver cable car from a trip to San Francisco) for my bracelet the previous Christmas. My mother asked me to quickly run back inside my grandmother's house to get my charm bracelet so our cousin would see me wearing it in church.

Southern etiquette.

I jumped out of the car, ran up the stairs of the porch, through the unlocked door, and toward the bedroom where my bracelet was. I hurried so that we wouldn't be late for church. I tripped over the door sill running into the bedroom and landed with my full weight directly on my right knee. I heard a crack and felt a pop. Unable to stand up, I crawled on my side to the bed and pulled myself up onto it. I lay there listening to my father honking the horn. Finally, one of the adults came in to see where I was. My knee was swelling rapidly and turning bright red. I tried to explain what had happened. Whoever came in to check on me told me to rest, and they would be back after church. The church was very close by, only a mile or so away, but it felt like they were gone for a very long time. It seemed weird that they had left me, but I was in too much pain to worry about that. I found that if I just didn't move at all, it didn't hurt too much. I had never been injured before, so all I knew was to just do whatever didn't hurt. I concentrated on not moving.

When my family came home from church, I was still on the bed in the same position. I wouldn't let anyone touch my knee. My grandmother called her doctor at home that Sunday afternoon, and he told her to have my parents bring me to his office. When my parents came to tell me, I told them I could not move. I had no idea how I would go to the bathroom, much less walk. My father reached down for me and very carefully carried me piggy back down the porch stairs to our car. It was the first time anyone had carried me in years.

While my grandmother looked after my sisters, my father, my mother, and I rode down a bumpy, quiet country road to reach my grandmother's doctor's office, which was in the house where he lived. My father gently carried me up the stairs and into his office, while I concentrated on not moving. The doctor was a kind, elderly man with round, wireless glasses and brown hair. He put his hand on my shoulder and lifted me onto an antique x-ray table in a room off the hall. A few minutes later, he showed us an image of my knee, white on black. He touched the picture where my knee cap was and told us it was broken into several pieces, like a puzzle. He told us he would splint my leg, but that we would need to go back home to Texas to see an orthopedic specialist since he was a general practitioner. My parents looked at each other with concern in their eyes. The doctor then said we needed to cancel our planned week at the beach to go directly home the next day. He gave us a piece of paper with his phone number on it and said the orthopedist could call him. He told my parents that I should eat ice cream.

And so the next day, my family got into our station wagon ready to make the journey home. My parents were in the front seat, while I sat with my right leg splinted and extended across the entire back seat, and my three younger sisters piled in the way back with all the luggage. We drove west all that day and most of the night to get home.

I eventually saw the orthopedic specialist in our hometown, was casted with a full leg cast, and spent half the summer waiting for the "puzzle pieces" of my kneecap to grow back together. Sometime in early July, the doctor used an electric saw to cut the cast off of my leg. My leg had been casted for six weeks and was now pale white with black hairs growing. I couldn't bend my knee, so I was instructed to sit on the kitchen counter several times a day and work to get my knee to bend.

When I completed physical therapy, my parents sent me to a summer camp in Colorado for four weeks. This was a surprise to me, and I wasn't at all sure that my knee would be okay so far from home. I will always remember arriving at the camp near the Rocky Mountains and meeting my cabin mates, just as I will always remember the horse I was assigned to ride. It was belonging—belonging to the other campers, to the kind and encouraging counselors, and to this beautiful and patient horse named King—that helped me heal. I came to trust my body again in the company of nature in the mountains of Colorado. Belonging brought me wholeness.

I still have trouble with this knee sometimes, almost fifty years later, all because I was in a hurry.

I was in a hurry to get the bracelet from my room in my grandmother's house.

I was in a hurry to do what my parents asked.

I was in a hurry to please our cousin by wearing the charm she had given me.

At the age of eleven, I knew how to be careful, but I hurried instead. The weeks of pain and limited movement and disappointment that followed were the first times I thought that maybe being a little slower wouldn't be so bad. Maybe I didn't have to prove my speed and my willingness to obey and to please everyone so much. What would happen if I slowed down and paid attention to myself? My bones had something to say to me. It wouldn't be the last time, but it would be a long time before I learned to listen.

Two days before I started medical school in Galveston, I was running up the steps of my building and missed a step, turning my ankle in the process. I heard a pop and crack and felt a sharp pain in my foot. I limped down the stairs to my room and lay on my bed, asking my roommate for some ice to put on my foot.

The next morning, my leg was bruised and swollen all the way to my knee. It hurt like crazy. I was so scared. A classmate who lived in my building came to check on me and offered to take me to the emergency room on his motorcycle. I hobbled to his bike, climbed on the back, and went to the ER, where an x-ray showed that the bone on the outside of my foot was broken. They put a cast on my foot and leg and told me to stay out of the water. They gave me crutches and told me to not bear any weight on that foot. I couldn't believe that after all the work I'd put in to get to medical school, I had done this.

The day after I broke my foot, classes started. My friend drove me to class on his motorcycle and carried my books. I was not very graceful, so my crutches made me lurch from side to side as I tried to hop on my other leg. I will never forget staring at the cadaver in my gross anatomy class that day. She smelled of formalin, and my own leg would smell like that for the whole first semester.

I saw the orthopedic doctor monthly, but my foot did not heal. I stayed on crutches and in a smelly cast for the entire first semester. My friend was an absolute lifesaver. We studied together every single night, like monks in a monastery. Every day, he drove me to class on his bike and then back home. Amazingly, we both survived the first semester and did well in our classes. At Christmas break, I was told to spend my vacation only on a couch or in bed. If my foot did not start to heal, they would perform a bone graft. This terrified me.

My foot healed over Christmas as I did nothing for three weeks but lie on the couch at my parents' home. I had a lot of time to think about how I'd missed that step months earlier in the first place. I had been in a hurry, and I wasn't paying attention. I felt anxious at the time, as though if I didn't hurry all the time, I would somehow miss something. It would take yet one more broken bone years later for me to realize that the opposite was true. As my foot healed and grew strong, I gave thanks for my classmate—my friend—who drove me on his motorcycle, who studied with me, who was supportive and encouraging even as the stress of medical school increased over time. Belonging in this friendship and in the other friendships from medical school became precursors for eventually belonging as colleagues in the medical community. Our empathy was sensitive and experiential as we learned so many things in so many ways. Belonging here not only helped my foot heal, but helped me grow into the doctor I would become over the years.

Almost thirty years later, in the year following my mother's death, I broke my ankle in a fall at a restaurant when I missed the bottom step as we were leaving. I underwent surgery to stabilize it where they pinned three fractures. It was my first experience with general anesthesia. I drew a star on my left leg to be sure the surgical team would not operate on the wrong leg. I was so afraid. I asked if I would be able to walk again. The answer was "probably." I was non-weight bearing for almost six months, a seemingly endless time of forced vulnerability. As a patient in physical therapy for several months, I literally had to learn to walk again. I held my therapist's hand as I took the first tentative steps. Those long months of healing slowed me way down.

Over time, I came to understand that I had missed the bottom step for a simple reason: Walking out of the restaurant, I had seen a sign on the door saying, "We smoke turkeys for Thanksgiving." My mind had immediately leaped to planning Thanksgiving dinner. But it was only May 31. My not being present in the moment caused me to miss the step and fall. For the third time in my life, I had suffered a significant broken bone because I was in a hurry. I knew deep inside that something badly needed to change.

I needed to pay attention. I needed to hear the message my body had been sending me my whole life. I needed to know what I wanted, and not focus so much on what would help everyone else. I needed to stop hurrying to please others, and I needed to stop getting hurt. Finally, I chose to look deep within my own spirit and ask again for understanding, this time asking myself, "What do you want?" I didn't have clear answers, but I came to believe the question was in fact holy and critical to living my life as I was called to live it.

As my ankle started to heal, I was referred to a physical therapist. I saw the therapist for almost six months. Years later, I believe that it was my conscious decision to collaborate with physical therapy as much as I could that gave me hope that I could recover, that I would walk again, and that I would be able to practice yoga again. My therapist was encouraging and supportive and offered challenges that kept me engaged, trying hard, and working hard. This team of professionals became my support team and I belonged to this clinic with a special devotion. The therapists and their assistants all came to know me. This group applauded when I took those first steps and understood how important it was to me to be as independent as possible. I remember how grateful I was the first time I was able to get up from the floor by myself. I belonged to this clinic and I belonged to myself more and more as my recovery progressed. Belonging was a key factor in my recovery and helped me tolerate the mystery of a lengthy and uncertain outcome. Belonging supported my desire to heal. Belonging became both my celebration and my touchstone.

When I returned to work after my ankle healed, I was far less accommodating. I felt compelled to openly confront whatever conflict existed among our team and within our system. Something about my ankle fracture dramatically decreased my willingness to tolerate deception, to tolerate disrespect. Our public mental health system was woefully underfunded and became more so each passing year. Even so, I decided to continue to speak out when decisions were made without appropriate input, to speak out when others were disrespected, to say very clearly what my recommendations were as the sitting medical director. I had found some kind of new mojo and enough energy to say louder what I had always said. I had found the courage to stop caring as much about how others perceived me, and to be seen as I was.

My desire was always to be a healer. Unfortunately, a lifelong practice of working to please others had repeatedly led to broken bones. My own bones spoke to my soul as I healed from all three fractures, and this was the mystery: How could I heal my own life?

I had always wanted to be a healer, but working to please everyone else had literally hurt me. I would need to reach beyond my own capacity in order to slow down, to listen, to pay attention. I needed to learn how to take care of myself, and I needed community to learn this. It was belonging that brought my healing, my step-by-step opening of my eyes to my own spirit.

May we listen to our desire to serve and follow where it leads. May we pay attention to the mystery, to what we don't know, and honor the space it takes to learn our own needs. May we always reach out to others for connection and community as we are led to healing and wholeness in the company of belonging.

Chapter 28

FEEDING MYSELF

"Deaf in one ear." This is what the note that I brought home from the school nurse in third grade said. I had failed the hearing test. Our pediatrician thought my hearing loss might be due to allergies, and so he referred me to an allergist in Dallas, a hundred miles away from home.

This was a mixed blessing. My mother and I got to ride the train (which I loved!) and I had her full attention for two days. We stayed in a downtown hotel, rode taxis, and saw a movie in the evening at the theater next door. But I was horrified by the allergy testing itself—ninety-six hypodermic needles on a silver tray and ninety-six injections in my arms. Twenty-four in each arm in the morning and again in the afternoon. I counted each one.

The next morning, the allergist delivered his verdict: "No cheese, no chocolate, no pepper (including no prepared meats like hot dogs), no oranges, no peaches, no feathers (no family bird)." And weekly allergy shots. And come back next year to be tested again.

This was a lot to absorb. Cheese was my favorite food. It was a Robinson family staple and had been for generations. I loved chocolate. And peaches and oranges were my favorite fruit. How could this be?

I would get used to this diagnosis, as we get used to such things. I ate a pineapple sandwich for lunch at school. Later, in sixth grade, I would put these allergies to the test with the help of a school friend who encouraged me to "eat it anyway" by bringing me chocolate bars at recess. I ate chocolate almost every day, starting with little bites. Nothing bad happened, even when I ate half of my friend's chocolate bar. I confessed this to the allergist at my yearly visit, who stared at me but didn't comment. After four years, we stopped the shots, and I was told I could eat what I wanted. It was almost as if, except for the tiny, chronic bumps on my arms from the shots, it had never happened.

But the damage had been done. My relationship with food had become all about what I wanted and was told I couldn't have. What I desired and what I was denied. What I desired was not only what I wanted, it was what my whole family had eaten for generations. What I had been taught was the way to nourishment, both physically and emotionally. I was torn between my family's culture and my specialty doctor in Dallas. Who was right? Tradition and desire or science and medicine? Was I really deaf? I wondered many years later if maybe I just had too much ear wax. What if these tests, likely rudimentary at the time, were inaccurate? This doctor had given me the message that some foods could be "wrong." That food could be "dangerous." That what I liked might not be what was "right."

When I was a senior in high school, I experienced anxiety that felt like a stomach ache. It seemed to come out of nowhere, this stomach pain. It ached and made me feel miserable. My college applications were making me nervous. I didn't really want to go, and I didn't know why. I was a good student and ended up being ranked second, academically, in my class of seven hundred. And yet, my stomach hurt, most often in social situations where I was expected to eat.

I discovered that I felt less anxious when my stomach was empty. I learned to induce vomiting to achieve this emptiness. I would prepare for most social events by vomiting along with brushing my teeth and putting on makeup. I felt much calmer and more peaceful with an empty stomach. I would pretend to snack at the parties, but I only drank water. Even then, it was only sips. I felt happy and relaxed when my stomach was empty.

146

I never told anyone about the induced vomiting. When I had my pre-college physical, my pediatrician told me that my weight was "perfect" and that I should try to stay at that weight while at college. The last time anyone had mentioned weight to me was years before, when I was getting the allergy shots. I had grown skinny, and I was encouraged to eat a slice of white bread at bedtime since I had been deemed allergic to cheese and chocolate and other foods I might have otherwise chosen. Now, years later, it occurred to me that my doctor was warning me about gaining weight even though he said I was "perfect." My allergies had disappeared, but food was apparently still dangerous.

I had an unhappy freshman year at a small, private college before transferring to the University of Texas at Austin. Luckily, my desire triumphed in this land of Tex-Mex food and Jerry Jeff Walker music. I found joy in my psychology studies, in new friends who would become lifelong friends, and with a new faith community in an exuberant post-Vatican II Catholic student center served by Paulist priests.

Food became not only nourishment again, but now delight and even sacrament. I loved drinking beer while playing board games with friends or listening to live Austin music in small bars. I loved the tacos and enchiladas, deep-dish pizza and greasy hamburgers. I wasn't anxious, and my stomach never hurt. I never threw up. It was here that belonging in community supported my desire for food and celebration. My friends and I were facing our own transitions into adulthood. I remember thinking that I would be happy staying in Austin forever, even staying in college for as long as we could. At the time, leaving the university and leaving Austin seemed impossible. These friendships and this community and this belonging were all idyllic, but we knew that not everyone would be able to find work in Austin or to stay there. This time of belonging ultimately supported me and others as we grappled with the reality that our whole lives lying before us were in fact giant mysteries, huge unknowns.

During my first year after college, I worked for the Social Security Administration in a small town in east Texas. I lived alone. I don't remember how it started, but somehow I read about the Atkins diet. I became curious and decided to try it. I lost weight very quickly as I watched my urine test strips turn purple, indicating I was in self-induced ketosis and would lose weight "automatically" by not eating any carbohydrates. I was astonished that I could manipulate my body with this "science." Once again, I came to see food as risky and also optional. More than once, I came to wonder if desire itself was also dangerous.

This was a short-lived experience, as I soon moved back to Austin. I was back in my cozy, comfy, happy place, and back to following desire, back to holy and celebratory eating. Eating what I wanted, when I wanted, and how much I wanted. Coming home to myself again. But somewhere deep inside, the idea that food was dangerous was growing, as was the idea that maybe I shouldn't trust myself, that I didn't in fact know what was best for me. This idea was growing roots far below the Austin-induced joy and would wait to rise again within me.

Over the following years, I mostly enjoyed feeding myself. I had occasional twinges of self-doubt, but I figured everyone had those. I wandered through my twenties eating freely. And then along came marriage. I bought a wedding dress that I loved and that fit me. However, I started worrying whether it would still fit me on my wedding day. I was relieved when it did.

My next twist and turn happened when I became pregnant. I had prepared for pregnancy by losing weight so that I could gain the pregnancy pounds. From somewhere came this idea that if I did this, I could go through the whole having-a-baby experience without my body changing. I was a physician and knew better, but the wishing heart is powerful. What I don't remember is why it was so important to me that my body not change. I didn't realize on an intuitive level what I now know to be true: A changing body is the constant in a woman's life. My obstetrician told me in my second trimester that I wasn't gaining enough weight, and that I needed to eat more, not less. This was enough to dislodge all my worries for the time being. I had a happy, healthy baby and gloried in eating joyfully alongside my daughter each day.

When my daughter was two and had been weaned for a while, I found myself almost unconsciously seeking out and showing up at a weight loss program near my job. It seemed so simple. Follow the program and lose weight. I did this in secret, for the most part, going to weekly meetings on my lunch hour. I learned the tricks for weighing in, including always going to the bathroom before getting on the scale. I bought accessories at the meetings that promised hope for a "new me" and added to the company's profit margin. I remember a much older woman who always sat in the first row. She was in her 80's and said every week that this meeting was her "church" and that she had been coming for many years. I never thought that I would be in her seat. I lost weight over several months and hit my "goal." I was celebrated in the meeting for this. But it was only the beginning, and now I was hooked.

I participated in this program off and on—though, mostly on—for almost twenty years. I anticipated each release of new material and bought merchandise every year. I restricted my eating according to the current guidelines as best I could. I joined three different meetings over the years with three different leaders. I abandoned my own knowledge about food without even realizing it. I bought the program's rules, and that was how I fed myself. Or how I didn't. As life became more stressful, I clung even tighter to the promises of this group.

But nothing really changed. I stopped living this commitment but kept paying for it. My body felt separate from my mind and heart. Mentally, I was really busy with my stressful job, my commute, caring for aging parents, and being a wife and a mom. I had outsourced my body to the program. I thought that was enough to keep me righteously in the land of "good nutrition." I felt like I had all those childhood allergies again, except that I didn't. I restricted my eating in an effort to please my doctors. I was a doctor and knew how happy I felt when my patients felt better, so I wanted to be a good patient for my doctors too. The ironic thing was, my doctors were always positive and supportive. I think they wanted to be good doctors for me the way I wanted to be a good patient for them. I was lucky and privileged to have doctors who respected and liked me. But I kept spending money on the program as though it were a church tithe.

A few years ago, I came across a website for an online course called "Feast." I started following Rachel Cole and her teachings. Rachel's words resonated deeply within me. Words about self-trust and feasting on life and food. I began to wonder about my program. But it was such a part of my life, it felt like some kind of weird insurance.

I thought I could explore this issue by myself and started reading research about weight loss programs, including the relationships of participants' "successes" to the organization's profits. I had never thought about this organization making a profit. In reality, the diet industry is a multi-billion-dollar enterprise. In reality, almost all weight lost in proprietary programs is gained back within a few years. In reality, many participants gain weight in the long run, whether compliant or non-compliant with the program.

When I stopped working full time, I decided I didn't need to spend money on this program any longer. But it was harder than I expected to let go. I was afraid to stop, and I didn't know why. I read more of Rachel's online postings and began to explore the Health At Every Size (HAES) paradigm that she referenced. I also read other HAES writers. I decided I needed support to be able to change my own paradigm, and I enrolled in Feast.

I cancelled my membership in the weight loss program. I studied the Feast offerings daily. I read about self-compassion, about highly sensitive people, about coping with emotions, and about intuitive eating. I had read most of this material before in other forms, but in Rachel's hands, these concepts sprang to life for me. It all became very simple: Let go of the scale and trust yourself. I had a lot of unlearning to do, but Rachel and the Feast group were right beside me the whole way. I didn't weigh myself at home for an entire year. I ate what called to me when I was hungry. I learned to listen to my satisfaction signals and to let go when I felt them. I am still learning and expect that I will be for years.

Today, I love feeding myself. Feeding myself food and pleasure and a peaceful life. This has always been my desire and my joy. I think breastfeeding my child brought a joy that came close to this. The weight loss program I belonged to for over two decades absolutely stole that joy (as well as my money), all with complete cultural and societal approval and praise.

Now I know better. My desire, the deep desire to be whole, is sacred. When I engage with this desire, the mystery of uncertainty tags along. In my years in the weight loss program, I knew exactly how much I weighed every day. Now I don't know, so numbers are a mystery. I live in that mystery in clothes that delight my senses, in colors and softness and happiness. And it has been belonging—Rachel's community in Feast and Rachel's personal support—that brought me through this mystery to a different kind of knowing and feeding myself, that brought me home to my desire.

I could say that desire, mystery, and belonging were part of the program I belonged to for so many years. And they were. But that desire, to have a different body and paradoxically for my body to never change, was not really my authentic desire. It was a shallow desire born from misguided societal and cultural expectations. My deepest desire, to be wholly myself and a whole human being, was never served by that program. I found that this deepest desire was served by Feast and Rachel's community, for which I am so thankful.

My deepest desire now is to trust, moment-by-moment and day-by-day, to become whole in order to serve as I am called.

May we always remember that deep inside, we know what is best for us. May we stay true to that desire, may we live bravely into that mystery of unknown outcomes, and may we seek and find communities of belonging that nurture wholeness and peace and love.

DEATH AND LETTING GO

Chapter 29

DEATH AND LETTING GO

Finally, this last group of stories looks at death and letting go. Letting go and releasing loved ones, seasons of life, homes, relationships, and possessions. Death is inevitable, of course, and most things in our lives are impermanent. The cliché that change is the only constant has held great meaning for me as I have grown older. Again, we see in these stories the interplay of our companions of desire, mystery, and belonging as time passes and we encounter challenges of surrender.

The first story is **My Father: The Long and Tender Goodbye**. It tells of my father's journey with thyroid cancer over almost twenty years. His illness ushered in the caregiving era for myself, my sisters, and our families as we learned to care for our parents as they had cared for us in our childhood. This was the first loss in my immediate family of origin, and one which I had feared for a long time. As always, the attendant mystery brought surprises, many of which were welcome, as we did our best to be faithful to Daddy's desire and to our belonging to each other.

The story of my mother's final illness follows in **My Mother: Her Rocket Ship and Hurricane Ike**. She died four and a half years after my father died. Her story is different in many ways, but both of my parents' stories are alike in that in the end, theirs was—and is—a love story. They lived on desire and love for each other. They were courageous in the mystery, the times of uncertainty, and they belonged to each other and to the world they loved fiercely.

The last story is **Letting Go**. It follows the theme of release and surrender, focusing more on how we live our lives than how we approach our deaths. How do we let go of our treasures, our possessions, our ideas, our expectations? How can we let go of what we believe we need? How can we come to trust that we will have what we need, that what we have is enough, that we ourselves are enough? This is my journey. I believe it is part of the mystery as we find deeper and deeper desires as we age and come to belong to our own truths at last.

The desire for a good death, for release from all that binds us, for peace as we age. The mystery of not knowing that becomes much more real in the second half of life. The belonging that we might be challenged to find as our lives change, as we are called to change how we live, maybe where we live, and who we live with. In the end, we seek the grace to flow with the river of our lives. My prayer here is that we will know love all of our lives and that we will recognize the grace that can lead us home to ourselves, home to the Holy that never leaves us and waits with love and peace for us to say yes.

Chapter 30

MY FATHER: THE LONG
AND TENDER GOODBYE

My father was diagnosed with thyroid cancer in 1989. In 1992, the year I married Bob, it was found to have spread to his lungs despite attempts at treatment. In 2000, he became oxygen-dependent, and in 2001, he entered hospice care in my parents' home in Longview, TX. He would live another three years.

During those years, I would drive five hours to Longview every few weekends to check on him and my mother, who herself had mobility issues after having suffered breast cancer and two broken hips. My parents wanted to stay in their home despite our efforts and hopes that they might agree to move closer to us. My sister, a physical therapist who had lived in Colorado for twenty years, moved to live near us to help with Mother and Daddy's care.

Sometimes I would take my then-toddler daughter Katie along for the weekend trips. We would listen to Disney songs in the car and stop for Sonic fruit slushes along the way. I couldn't bear to not see her on the weekends when I went to Longview, so I brought her along. One December trip, when Katie was about five, my dad (who was still driving despite his care team's concerns) told her that he wanted her to help him deliver Christmas presents to my parents' friends. Katie quickly jumped up, very excited to be her Papa's helper. I stared at my father and said, "Daddy, I don't think this is a good idea. Why don't I drive you?"

He shook his head. "No, I am going to drive and take my beautiful granddaughter to deliver presents to my friends!" I looked at him again. His eyes were the same blue as hers. They both looked at me, silently pleading.

I had no idea how capable my weakened dad was of driving, but I could see how much they both wanted this time together. So I gave in, smiled (with a little bit of pretending) and said, "Let's go! I'll just ride in the backseat."

We all got in the car, my dad driving slowly but with great intention to each of his friends' homes. At each house, Katie took a wrapped gift and ran to the porch, leaving the present by the front door. She was so excited. My father beamed while watching her. I knew desire when I saw it. This was a love that was beyond my control, a love between grandparent and grandchild, a love surely smiled on by the Holy.

Another December, an ice storm threatened Longview. I called my parents the evening before it was due to arrive, asking them about the heat in their house. They assured me they would be fine; they had extra blankets, were warm, and not worried. When I woke up the next morning, I called them again before leaving for work. No answer. I waited a few minutes and called again. Still no answer. I knew my father woke up at 5:30 am as he loved to listen to the BBC news on the internet. I called a third time, but no one picked up.

My next call was to my supervisor, telling her I wouldn't be at work, that I was driving to Longview. I dressed warmly and set off on the five-hour drive. On the way, I called the electric power company in Longview. The person who answered told me that most local residential power was out due to the ice storm that had arrived in the night. I explained that my father used an oxygen concentrator and was dependent on electricity. The person told me that by law, they had fourteen days to restore the power. Fourteen days. I hung up and drove faster. Every thirty minutes, I called my parents... still, there was no answer.

After driving for four and a half hours, I was almost there. I was chilled, more by my fear than the outside temperature. All I could think about was the prospect of my parents, frozen to death in their bed, and the headlines that would read, "Psychiatrist's Parents Die of

Exposure in Ice Storm." I called my parents' phone number one more time. This time, my father answered. He brightly said, "Hello!" and asked me how I was doing. When I told him that I was twenty minutes away from Longview, he asked why.

"Don't you have to be at work?" he asked. I all but screamed that I had been calling him all morning. He said, "Well, we went to Jucy's for breakfast! We left the 'mobile phone' at home!" Jucy's was the local diner.

I asked, "What about your oxygen?"

He said, "Oh, I brought a portable tank but left it in the car... sometimes people light up a cigarette outside Jucy's." I almost drove the car off the road.

"Well, Daddy, I am coming to see you and Mother. I will be there soon."

He said, "Well, there was no need for that... but maybe you can pick up some hamburgers for lunch? With French fries?"

So I stopped and got burgers and fries. I sat with my mother and father in the house I grew up in and ate a hamburger. They asked me to stay overnight, but since their power was back on, I needed to go back to my job. Within a few years, I would lose both of them, but that day, they defeated the ice storm and my own catastrophic fears. I drove the five hours back home, oddly happy and almost euphoric with relief, singing Christmas carols with the radio all the way.

In the spring of 2004, the hospice doctor in Longview told us that they could no longer safely care for our father. My dad refused to allow "help" to come to their house at night, even though the doctor had assembled a robust team of daytime helpers for both him and our mother. My sisters and I had walked this long path with my parents, and now we were given no choice but to move them both to Houston immediately.

By some miracle, my sisters and their families were able to converge in Longview from across the country within a day, so we were able to collectively pack up the necessities for my parents. This made me cry.

We were surprised to learn that my dad had kept a pistol in his bedroom closet. He asked us to go get a box on the top shelf, and when we opened it for him, we saw the gun. He held it and waved it around a little. We stared at each other, stunned. We had never been a "gun family," although my dad grew up hunting ducks as a boy. My sister's boyfriend said, "That is a very nice gun!" We quickly surrendered that gun to the local police.

Before leaving Longview, we visited my dad's pharmacist for medication refills to bring with us, and that sweet, caring man told me, "There won't be any other men like your dad. He is a true gentleman," making me cry, again.

Daddy was transported in an ambulance to Houston with one of my sisters riding along. The rest of us followed behind with my mother and their things. We prayed together before leaving my parents' home of 44 years. I wasn't sure he would survive the trip. In fact, the ambulance attendants looked very worried, but five long hours later, we brought my parents into the same skilled nursing facility in Houston where my sister was employed. The administrators had shuffled beds and rooms so that my parents could stay in a room together, and we engaged a new hospice provider.

My father lived—miraculously, in my eyes—another three weeks. Each day was both agony and a miracle. At one point, exhausted, I asked his doctor, "Whatever happened to people dying in their sleep?"

One Thursday evening, my father woke up and asked my sisters and I what we were doing Saturday evening. When we told him we didn't have any plans, he smiled at us and went back to sleep.

Three days later, on Saturday evening, my husband and my daughter and I, all of my sisters and their families, and my best friend and her son were all gathered at my father's bedside when he quietly slipped away and died. This was a moment I had dreaded for many years, and I was so surprised that all I could sense in the room was light. I had spent the Friday night before at my father's bedside and was lost for hours in the mystery of this night. I kept my hand on his arm and shoulder. Around 3:00 am, the hospice nurse told me that she thought he was "actively" dying, and so I woke my mother as she had asked, and we sat close to him. An hour went by, and the nurse smiled at us and said, "Maybe not yet."

He waited, or God waited, who knows, until we were all together the next day. When the time finally drew near, my husband prayed from my little red Book of Common Prayer (page 465):

> *"Into your hands, O merciful Savior, we commend your servant Robbie. Acknowledge, we humbly beseech you, a sheep of your own fold, a lamb of your own flock, a sinner of your own redeeming. Receive him into the arms of your mercy, into the blessed rest of everlasting peace, and into the glorious company of the saints in light. Amen."*

I kept my hand over my father's heart as it slowed and finally stopped. I knew in those final moments that we were in the presence of only grace and light. I told my sister I could feel the energy of Daddy's spirit right above his head with my hand, and she felt it too.

I felt sad and also strangely relieved and thankful, relieved that he was no longer suffering and thankful that we had done our best to be faithful. I felt proud that somehow we were able to "see him safely home." I was grateful that, together, we had been able to realize our desire to accompany our father until that last moment of life and the first moment of the mystery of the life to come. We were surrounded by the light of the Holy and bathed in grace upon grace. I pray to always remember the presence of the sacred in that room and the gentleness and great love of my beloved father.

Chapter 31

MY MOTHER: HER ROCKET SHIP AND HURRICANE IKE

In September of 2008, my mother was eighty years old. It was the middle of hurricane season, and one weekend, concern arose about the possibility of Hurricane Ike becoming a threat to the Houston-Galveston area. The Monday morning before Ike hit, my sister Kathy called me at my job. She said my mother had said to her earlier that morning, "Hi Kathy, today I am going up in a rocket ship." This was not my mother's usual style of conversation. Because of concern that my mother might be delirious from some infection or other cause, she was taken to the emergency room. I left work and joined her and Kathy there.

My mother was conscious and, as always, pleasant, although she seemed weak. She told us that she was feeling fine. The emergency room staff seemed puzzled by her weakness. Her blood pressure was low. The emergency room nurse said that maybe the blood pressure cuff "just wasn't working right." I told the nurse I was worried about her low blood pressure and what might be causing the drop. In the past, low blood pressure had heralded serious infections requiring hospitalization, so I asked about her lab results.

At lunchtime, the staff brought my mother a tray. I helped her eat lunch, feeling all the while that something very wrong was happening. My mother ate the whole plate of food and said, "It was good!" Shortly after finishing her lunch, quietly and without fanfare, my mother slipped into unconsciousness. She was quickly taken upstairs to the ICU and placed on a ventilator to help her breathe.

We weren't allowed to see her for the next several hours as the ICU team remained in her room, working hard. My husband Bob and my sister sat in the waiting room with me. It was also the day of our daughter Katie's seventh grade open house, so I would later ask Bob to leave and go to the junior high event. My feet were glued to the ICU waiting room floor. After a couple of hours, the doctor came out to tell us that my mother was "stabilizing" but still very fragile. He asked if we wanted CPR performed if her heart stopped. Bob looked at me and said, "You know what your dad would say." I told the doctor no, that we wanted her to be comfortable. This all felt so unreal. I kept thinking about what my mother meant by talking about going on a rocket ship that morning. Did she have some sense of what might happen, or was it just random chatter?

Meanwhile, the hospital staff kept talking about Hurricane Ike. I knew that the hospital might have to evacuate, and I knew that we might need to evacuate from our home. We still hadn't seen our mother, and Katie was home alone while Bob was at her open house. I told my sister I was going home to check on Katie, and I would be back. I called Katie and told I would be there soon. She said she was hungry and asked for McDonald's, so I pulled through the drive-thru and brought her dinner. When I got home, I sat on the couch with her and told her that Grandma Kate was very sick. She listened carefully as she ate her fast food dinner. I had only been home from the hospital for a few minutes when my sister called me and said that the nurses were asking me to come back.

My mother had not regained consciousness by the time I got back to the hospital. Her heart rate was slowing despite multiple medications to maintain it. When I arrived, I went straight to her room in the ICU, as they now allowed us to be in the room with her. I stood by her bed and held her hand and stroked her hair. I kept telling her, "You are so beautiful, thank you for loving us so well." Over and over, "so beautiful." She was so beautiful.

Her heart gradually slowed and stopped. The doctors had told us that CPR had almost no chance of reviving her, and that even if it did, she would not leave the hospital alive. So, as with my dad when he died four years earlier, I felt sad and overwhelmed. But even in the chaos of the ICU, I sensed light in the room. I thanked God for my mother's life. Somehow in that moment, I believed, as my mother had, that all would be well. I sure didn't know how, and certainly not with a Category 4 hurricane approaching. But my mother's willingness to consent to mystery and to at last allow herself to surrender to her desire for the Holy gave me the strength to move forward through the following days, during which we evacuated before Hurricane Ike hit and held her memorial service in Longview.

The days were a blur of rapid travel arrangements. We drove north through surface level clouds and lashing rain as if through a cloud of locusts from a Biblical plague. We had to stay in a different hotel each night in Longview because the hurricane exodus had filled most hotel rooms. My sisters had to fly into Dallas rather than Houston. When the funeral home informed us that my mother could not be buried due to the approaching storm and that they would need to bury her at a later date, I felt horrified but helpless.

Instead of a graveside service, we sat in the funeral home chapel for a few prayers with a local minister. I told him that I was worried about the planned memorial service at my parents' church. I was afraid that my parents' elderly friends would come to the service and somehow be harmed by the storm, but he told me the church had candles and lanterns ready if the electricity went out. So, as we had for my father, we gathered later in St. Andrew Presbyterian Church, where my parents' lifelong friends came and worshiped, celebrating my mother's life as they had my father's a few years earlier. There was beautiful music, and there were simple prayers. There was a lovely reception where my sisters and I were embraced by childhood friends and their families. No one seemed worried about Hurricane Ike.

As it turned out, Ike did come to Longview, and we huddled in local hotels for a few days. That same weekend, my husband's beloved aunt, who had been ill with cancer for months, died in Ohio. Bob and Katie and I kept driving further north, all the way to Cincinnati to sit in another funeral home and remember his aunt, who was also his godmother. We had brought all our treasures from our house that we could fit in the car as well as the legal documents I knew I would need for the funeral home. I had been afraid to leave these treasures and documents in case Hurricane Ike caused flooding in our neighborhood and destroyed them. It was a terribly sad few weeks. We looked and felt like refugees.

A few days after we returned home, our beloved, elderly golden retriever died. He had stayed with my friend Beverly and her family during the hurricane, but returned to us when we came home. Our hearts were broken. The loss of sweet Max felt unbearable. I felt like I would never stop grieving. The day I returned to work, I walked into the building and burst into tears. I couldn't stay in my office, so I just went home. It would be weeks before things would feel "normal" again. My sisters and I were orphans now.

I have thought to myself many times, "Whose mother dies in the shadow of a hurricane?" And the answer comes, "The same person whose mother dressed a mannequin in the window at Halloween to delight all the trick or treaters, who made sure that every member of our extended family, including husbands and grandchildren, had the same handmade Christmas stocking as the ones that we had hung since childhood." My mother's life was not easy. But her last few years were glorious in many ways. She surprised us all with her newfound resilience after my father died. I was learning that sometimes death brings surprises.

Like many physicians—like many adult children—I am much more comfortable in life if I have some semblance of control. I did everything I could to try and do "the right thing" in taking care of my parents. I don't think I realized until they died that they'd had their own journeys to travel... they for sure had their own relationships with the Holy and their own invitations at the end of their lives. I wanted so badly—and worked so hard—to do all I could to help them, and while they were always very appreciative, they were clearly experiencing their own encounters with desire and mystery in the final days of their lives. Any sense of control I had was only an illusion.

This story was not about me. Both of my parents were fully themselves as they let go of life, as they said goodbye. I was thankful to be with both of them, knowing that even though they very much loved us and loved life, they turned toward the Holy with great love and surrender. I learned much from this time, and a lot of it was how futile my worry and fretting were in the end.

In the end, I began to understand this: If we turn away from mystery, we will never know our true desires, and we will never be fully ourselves, fully whole. We cannot know our deepest desires without consenting to mystery. We survive the unknowable—even the unimaginable—by always embracing the deep desires of our heart. This crossroad of desire and mystery is where the Holy waits for us all of our lives. It's a belonging that transcends anything we can possibly imagine.

Chapter 32

LETTING GO

There is a story in the Gospels about Jesus taking three friends up on a mountain. While they were there, Jesus became transfigured and "his face shone like the sun and his clothes became dazzling white" (Matthew 17:2). Suddenly, Moses and Elijah appeared and began talking with Jesus. Peter, one of Jesus' friends, became excited and said he would build three houses there on the spot, one for Moses, one for Elijah, and one for Jesus. The story goes on to say that then God spoke from a bright cloud, saying, "This is my Son, the Beloved; with him I am well pleased; listen to him" (Matthew 17:5). Awed, Peter wanted to freeze this moment in time. It couldn't get any better than that. I always found common ground with Peter.

I don't like letting go. It is hard for me. Transitions have never been easy, and although I understand well that change is the only constant in life, I still fret about releasing anything. I have many books about decluttering, and yet I still have most of my work material in our study even though I retired a few years ago.

I want to stop time. In the absence of holding on to people, I hold on to their stuff. It is hard to say goodbye. But though I know that the things are not the people to whom they belonged, I still have this sense that somehow the stuff is alive. That releasing other people's things can hurt them. That things can protect me—from what, I don't know. None of this is true. I don't think that all the books in the world about decluttering can teach me to stop time.

But why would I even try to stop time?

Letting go of the old makes space for the new. We move from the past to the present to the future. As the present becomes the past, that is where I might clutch and choke. I think I need the things (and people and events and places) of the present that are now becoming the past to sustain me in the future that is not yet here. I know this logic doesn't make sense, and yet its hold on me is very strong.

Learning to release is important. Learning to flow is important, and maybe especially so in the second half of life. Every time we let go, we practice freedom. When I was a child, my family would go to Six Flags Over Texas, an amusement park in Dallas. There was a giant tree there that had a spiral slide inside it. You climb the tree to the top and then slide down in a spiral on the inside. The first time I tried this attraction, the speed of the downward slide scared me. I pushed out my arms to try and slow myself down a little. I felt burning in my elbows. When I came out of the bottom of the slide, I had giant blisters on both elbows and arms. The slide was metal, and the friction had raised blisters on my skin. I think that life is kind of like that slide: If we hold back too much or hold on too tight, we end up with blisters on our spirit. It takes courage to let go, but there actually isn't much choice. Life overflows with transitions, and nothing on earth—no "stuff"—can stop them.

Peter wanted time to stop. It was illogical and didn't happen, but he still wanted it. Our loved ones die. When I was younger, I realized that every relationship I had would end with the death of either me or the other person. The only way I would escape having to let go of everyone I knew was if I died first. This seemed terribly unfair. We have to release and let go. It is an important skill, and one of the hardest for me. So how can we practice this skill of releasing, of letting go, that is so essential to us for flowing into the future? How can I help myself release what is no longer necessary? What keeps me from the liberation of letting go?

We all die. As I get older, death seems more familiar. But it can still be hard to actually imagine. These things I know:

We are called not to control, but to trust;

We know more than we think we do;

Help is available; and
Love goes on.

When my father decided to accept hospice care, I felt a huge urge to control things, to impact the situation and make decisions, to be a doctor instead of a daughter. I have learned that left to my own devices, I would have done it all wrong. His decision to stay at home while he could bought us time, abundant time, precious and amazing time. It taught me about distance and separation, and it has shown me the illusion of control and the blessing of surrendering to grace. The challenge is that even if we believe, magic won't always happen. Some people may be cured, but most are not. Yet if we believe, we will be led by courage and hope—in this life and the life to come. To let go, trust, and believe—these are the elementary lessons of not wasting energy in the pursuit of control, of leaving the door open to love. We don't know what will happen, but if we live each day content with not knowing, we will be free until the day death comes.

Finally, I have learned that love—and life—goes on. It is possible in life to give yourself to your children and live on in them. I am more conscious now of my grandparents' DNA inside me—not just the color of my eyes or how tall I am, but my strengths and passions and personality, all inherited from them. I choose now to trust and believe that my parents will live on in me as long as I live, and they (and I) will live on in my daughter when I am no longer here. It is, in fact, more than genetics. It is a spiritual legacy—prayer that becomes cellular in another person's body. It is willed love that imprints into molecules of blood and bone and brain. It is who we are and who we become and, in the end, who we give to the world.

I found my way through the deaths of my parents. Writing helped. Not wanting them to suffer helped. Close relationships with my sisters helped. The support of Bob and Katie helped. These were big transitions, one after the other. It has taken years to organize and distribute their possessions, and I am still working on it. I hold the books that my parents read and loved, and it is hard to let go of them. But my parents are not in their books. We let go of people in our lives, willingly or unwillingly. Their possessions might help us remember them, but they are not present in the possessions. While my logical brain understands this, my emotional brain falters at times and wants to hold on, to build a house, to stop time.

Releasing people teaches us grace. Releasing things gives us space. Releasing ourselves into the flow of time offers us freedom from the blisters of trying to force everything to slow down.

In the transfiguration story of Jesus, Matthew's gospel tells us this: "When the disciples heard this (God's voice from the cloud saying that Jesus was his beloved son), they fell to the ground and were overcome by fear. But Jesus came and touched them, saying, 'Get up and do not be afraid'" (Matthew 17:6-7). These were not the last words of Jesus in this story, but they are the words that stick with me.

Get up and do not be afraid.

I heard a priest at the University of Texas Catholic Student Center preach about this passage years ago, and I have never forgotten what he said: We are called to get up, and we are called to not be afraid.

We can and must surrender to the flow of time and nature. If we are lucky enough to live for a long time, we will age. All parts of us will age. Life goes on. Love goes on. We don't exist in our possessions. We will be remembered in the hearts of those who love us and in the DNA of those who remain.

When he was near death, my father told us not to worry—that he might die, but he would still be present on the earth. He went on to say that each of his four children had 50% of his DNA, or in total, we had two complete copies of his DNA. His five grandchildren each had 25% of his DNA, or a total of one and a quarter copies of his DNA. He smiled at us as he said that even after he died, there would remain three and a quarter complete copies of his DNA walking around on the planet.

Our existence is limited, and the veil between us and those we've lost is thin. The liminal, transitional space of death brings everything we release together again. It is okay to let go. It is important to let go. And as we do, the Holy holds everything and everyone for us so that no love is ever abandoned, and no treasure is left behind.

May we recognize our desire to hold on as an invitation to trust more in the holiness of life. May we escape the blisters of attempting to control the mysteries we live in all our days. And may we walk together, belonging to each other, sharing life and love, so that our spiritual DNA is shared between us just as physical DNA is shared in families. And when we ourselves let go for the last time, there will be innumerable copies of our DNA remaining on the planet to live on in the love we have shared together.

DESIRE, MYSTERY, BELONGING AGAIN

Chapter 33

DESIRE, MYSTERY,
BELONGING AGAIN

We have traveled through these seven areas of life: love, work, family, grace, creativity, healing and wholeness, and death and letting go. We have seen the presence of desire, mystery, and belonging in each of these areas in the stories shared here. These are my stories, my perceptions, and my memories. As noted earlier, as you read my stories, or any other stories, they may inspire reflection on your own stories, perceptions, and memories. I chose to focus on desire, mystery, and belonging; others might have different descriptors and approaches to looking at their lives.

Desire, mystery, and belonging called to me, not just individually, but also in how I experienced them in relationship to each other. Understanding this interplay as I listen to others' stories has helped me come to see our unique ways of being, both as individuals and in all that we share in our common humanity.

Together, desire, mystery, and belonging create a rhythmic pattern that we can come to remember and recognize. We can recall how we have seen these experiences that are present in our own lives before moving toward an understanding of how these experiences are not only present, but engage with each other, in others' lives.

We come to see that some days, we are aware of desire, of delight, and of joy. Some days, we are aware of the mystery of all that we do not know, and of anxiety and sadness. Our practice and awareness of belonging can sustain us through all of this—through the desire and through the mystery—as we learn to engage with our lives and our world with thoughtfulness, with intention, with respect, and with love.

This is one way to explore our lives and reflect on our experiences. There are countless other ways. This book offers one path, acknowledging that we choose from many paths each day.

Finally, this reflection invites looking ahead. We come to understand the past through reflection and memory. We walk through our present days with presence and awareness. We can also come to practice hope as we learn to trust in the desire that is love, the mystery that we experience as our crucible, and the belonging that teaches us to be faithful. It is all of this together that makes a life, which brings us home to who we are and to who we might become.

Chapter 34

ALL TOGETHER: DESIRE, MYSTERY, BELONGING

And so we return again to these three movements of life we have explored. Desire, mystery, and belonging live in our garage, in our bathroom, in our refrigerator, and in our closet. These three companions travel together. They are always ready for adventure, and they always invite us forward. For some years now, I have begun to look for them, separately and together, in whatever circumstances I meet. They are concrete in our everyday experience, and they will outlive us on this earth.

I have shared stories in different realms of life about the movements of desire, mystery, and belonging, all in the context of a larger spiritual journey. I have looked at love, work, family, grace, creating, healing, wholeness, and death and letting go. I can look back and see the role of desire in these stories as well as the roles of mystery and belonging. If we choose, we can look at all of our stories and see desire, mystery, and belonging all at play together.

I imagine them as a spiral. Desire leads to mystery that leads again to desire, while belonging is the chain that joins desire and mystery. The spiral of this movement can travel up or down, sideways, or even inside out. This movement is about seeking and following the Holy in the context of our own lives, our own everyday experiences. When we orient to the Holy, imperfectly as we do, we align our intentions and energy with grace. When we need to make a decision, we discern what is best by measuring our outcome against a touchstone or a benchmark.

Desire, Mystery, and Belonging

Desire, mystery, and belonging all have their place here; when we are aware of them, we become conscious of our choices. Our values and our hopes and dreams all matter when we recognize our deepest desires, become well-acquainted with mystery, and support our journey with belonging and community.

When we can recognize them retrospectively, the next invitation is to consider them prospectively. For many years, I thought that my deepest desires would "have to wait." I thought they might be related to things that could be bought with money or things that I couldn't control, like whether someone loved me or approved of me or not. It took a long time for me to integrate Bonaventure's, "If you want to know God, follow your deepest desire." Since we are made in God's image and likeness, we have God within us. So if our deepest desire is planted by the Holy, then once we discern it, we can indeed nurture and grow it. We can learn to be our most authentic selves with the help of our better angels. We can ask ourselves, "What do I really want, what is really calling to me now?"

Once we discern our true desire in the moment—our deepest desire—we can anticipate the mystery that will follow as we seek our desire. Instead of waiting until all conditions are right and ready (which is never), we understand that there may and will be complications and stumbling blocks we could not anticipate. This is the mystery, and it happens whether we are ready or not. All desires, great and small, can be thwarted by unanticipated mystery. The question is whether we give up in resignation (and maybe a bit of self-pity), or we anticipate how we might respond to any roadblocks. We lengthen and broaden our perspective even as we commit more deeply to our desire. We can welcome the challenges that arise as an invitation to learn more about ourselves and about our desire and our commitment to it. When we persevere and creatively trouble-shoot these challenges, we find our desire waiting for us just beyond the next curve in the road. We understand that this renewed desire might, and likely will, lead us into mystery, but we consent to this as we lean toward alignment with our true selves and with the Holy.

As always, the closest path between desire and mystery and desire again is belonging. Community can support us in the joy and in the sorrow of life. The temptation is to try to be independent, to figure things out for ourselves. A commitment to belonging in advance of the decision to pursue any specific desire is like insurance. There will be times when we are not sure, when we feel lost, when we want to turn back and think that we made a mistake. More often than not, these times arise from the mystery that is the foil of desire, the balancing force to everything we want. Belonging in community provides us with a place to vent, to question, and to ask why. Different companions have different strengths, and so in any community, we have access to a diversity of resources. When we are willing to share our struggles as well as our celebrations, we can access new ideas, new strategies, and simple empathy that can re-energize us on our journey and help heal our doubts. Belonging leads us from desire to mystery and back again to desire.

Belonging is the swinging bridge that we cross with others over the chasm between two peaks.

I discerned a deep desire to write this book, to write it in a voice that might encourage the reader to explore their own spiritual path with desire, mystery, and belonging. I felt a call to write this book, to offer the reader a glimpse of spiritual reflection and perhaps a clearer sense of spiritual direction via a new lens: the lens of desire, mystery, and belonging. I wanted to connect with readers and to do it by writing. The first time I sat down to write, I might have lasted ten minutes at the most before deciding that I was thirsty and needed a drink, that I was lonely and needed to call a friend, or that I was tired and needed to take a nap. That's the mystery, right there. I am cut off from my desire to write, and any movement toward that desire is thwarted by the simplest obstacles of thirst, of loneliness, of sleepiness. Underneath might lie the obstacles of fear, of doubt, of lack of self-trust. These could have successfully stopped me in the first chapter, but for belonging.

It was a writing group, writing retreats, a writing coach, fellow writers who would exchange pages with me, and telling loved ones I was writing that made the difference. These communities, large and small, supported and carried me through the mysteries over and over again back to my desire to write. And instead of one chapter, I have almost completed a manuscript as I type these words.

It sounds obvious and deceptively simple: Know what you want and go after it. However, nuances arise in mystery and belonging—it's important to understand that deep desire does not equal superficial desire. New shoes are nice, but they are not necessarily a way to know God.

This becomes a practice, then, and we can choose to integrate these movements consciously into our daily lives as well as into any major transition.

Discern and follow your deepest desire.

Allow and consent to mystery, imperfection, and ambiguity.

Seek belonging and community for both support and clarification along the way.

When we consciously follow this path and ask these questions, the Holy waits for us and walks beside us. We can choose to pay attention to our lives and the moments of these movements that emerge day to day. We can agree to say yes to the Holy even as the seeds of our deepest desire are gently planted while we sleep.

When I can turn toward my deepest desire and follow it—rather than deferring it or settling for more superficial desires—I learn thankfulness and gratitude for my own unique gifts that I can share rather than hide. When I can accept mystery and tolerate ambiguity rather than acceding to the self-doubt of not knowing it all, I learn to hope for the best outcome for all. When I engage in belonging, I move from isolation and brokenness to healing and wholeness, healing as an individual myself, and wholeness within myself and in the larger community.

May we turn again and again to the desires that nestle in our deepest knowing, our deepest selves, and may we welcome them. May we trust ourselves in the mysteries as we grow into the knowledge that our common humanity ensures that we will stumble and fall. May we hold belonging and community as the treasure that offers us courage, that offers us insight, that offers us love that will always feed us on our journey—this journey in this life and in the life to come.

Chapter 35

In the End:
A Benediction

This book is about desire, mystery, and belonging as a path to the Holy. What do we want in a spiritual journey? Bonaventure says, "If you want to know God, follow your deepest desire." Another way to think about this is to be the most "me" that we can each be—the most Sarah, the most you, the most whoever. What I, the writer, want is to be able to trust myself in the vicissitudes of life. To have a steady inside that can withstand buffeting from the outside. To orient to my desire as to a light that shines in the darkness. To have a touchstone, even if I don't think I will ever fully understand it. To belong to the beloved and to the stranger, to those I know and to those I will never meet—to belong to the human race. To fully take life in and to fully let life go. To not stop time (as if I could). To show up, and in showing up as me, to always remember what lies beyond my knowing: the energy of the Holy, of life itself. It doesn't all depend on me. It never did. But I can walk with desire into the mystery, knowing that I am loved, and know grace and mercy along my path. I can surrender to belonging to myself and to the Holy, to living deeply in community, in radical communion. In the end, what we have left is love and grace. What I want is to live close to my deepest desire, knowing that devotion is another face of Love.

This book really has no ending because desire, mystery, and belonging are often cyclical. And so at the end of this story, we can turn back to the beginning, and continue to journey as long as we have breath. So what happens when someone follows her deepest desire and consents to mystery and allows herself to belong in community? What kind of life does this lead to?

I believe that she knows what she knows. Not just the facts and what to do when someone has chest pain and how to make chocolate sheet cake and the fastest way to drive into Houston. She knows what her body is telling her. She pays attention to the voice of the Holy speaking in nature and in her relationships. She slows down. She can listen to others for a long time, and she hears the mystery and the desire in their voices. She loves to go for walks. She is not afraid of what may come because she trusts herself to show up as who she is, and that who she is will know the way. Who she is will listen for what rings true. She will do the best she can, and then she will rest. When she feels sad, she will cry. She will laugh with the children and hold babies, and she will pray in the morning and at night. She serves others, as a healer and as a friend. She will learn how to let go with an open heart, knowing that desire is like the moon and has cycles of waxing and waning. She will make new stories when the old stories feel too small or too dishonest.

She walks away from what is false, from what is violent, from what is too much to hold, carry, or bear. She still wants to make a difference, but now she knows that she doesn't have to exhaust herself helping others. She remembers to rest, and she loves to create. She keeps lots of books, music, and art supplies around her house. She doesn't worry about cleaning out her closet. She gives herself a break. She listens for the secrets of the angels. She knows that life may always be too short, but that love is eternal. She believes what her college roommate once said: "Nothing is waste that makes a memory." She knows that forgiveness is holy and that kindness is sacred.

There is so much we can never know. In the end, we have the choice to just be who we are as we follow the light of our deepest desire. When we say yes, we walk on the path of mystery, but we do not walk alone. Grace leads to wholeness and wholeness leads to redemption. As we honor our deepest desire and as we consent to be who we are in the mystery of life, we reclaim all that we are and all we have ever been and all that we will be. And in the end, we will take our place in the stars in the sky or in the morning sunbeams, knowing that in good times and in bad, we lived in truth and walked in love all the days of our lives.

And so we arrive into mystery yet again. Each part of our lives invites us again into mystery, into belonging, into desire. Birth itself is a mystery, and yet, while still attached to our mother, we utter the cry of desire.

We come into the world cradled with our own history. We are who we are in our DNA. The prayers and love and wishes for our well-being are etched in our bones along with the pain and horror of trauma. There are stories in our families, stories of loss and stories of triumph. We learn who we are in these stories. We look in the mirror and see our ancestors staring back, perhaps smiling at us. We learn about the Holy, either because we are told or because we are not told... either way, there is a sense of the beyond just behind our eyes.

We are welcomed either kindly or cruelly. Sometimes, we are ignored. If we are lucky, we begin to tell our own stories, even as children, to our brothers and sisters, to ourselves, to the angels, to the wind. We learn belonging, in all of its joy and possibility. We learn the ways of our people and their connection to the Holy.

We begin to be challenged as adolescents and young adults to take our place in the world of work. To have a vocation. To hear a call. It is here that the Holy whispers most tenderly, so softly that it is easy to miss. Law school, medical school, seminary, marriage, celibacy, all of these vocations. To hear the call of the Holy, we need to listen. The world laughs at this, but somehow we hear the call anyway. And we say yes, or we say no, or we say not yet, maybe later. But the call remains, and the invitation persists, the desire, the belonging, and the mystery.

We are seen as adults when we create our world, our jobs, our homes, our families. We become responsible. Mystery seems to be our enemy at times—and speaking of time, who has time for desire? We might worship in a church, but how often are we given, how often do we ask for, or even demand, time for quiet? Time for listening to the Holy. Making a living, raising children, and being a grown-up all take time and so much energy. Sometimes we forget we have a choice.

Yet the Holy stands right behind us, sits in the passenger seat, singing a song into the flowers by the road.

And at last, or at some time, we are finally invited. Invited into the mystery of aging. Our bodies slow down, or in some cases, find new life. Sometimes we are now able at long last to care for ourselves—mind, body, and spirit. We negotiate relationships, and we find a path to slow down or stop working. We may begin to create, and the mystery becomes our friend. If we can allow the mystery, desire is almost always waiting for us again. We may paint or play the piano, play golf or take more naps. The next life may begin to interest us more. It may also frighten us, or we may not acknowledge any life other than this one. Even so, the beautiful afternoon light, ripples on a pond, glorious autumn leaves—these catch our breath in ineffable ways. Life can be so big.

So it is and will be with all our life. We may never comprehend how vast and wide this experience we call "life" is. We may come to know in time how much mystery moves us forward. How desire walks beside us, whispering in our ear each step, "One more, one more, one more." There is so much we don't know, may never know, and yet we already have and know everything we need.

The Holy finds us. It comes to us. The Holy is always and forever exactly right here.

And this is our benediction.

May we know this day and always the blessing of consenting to mystery. May we live in surrender to belonging. May we this day and always bless and heal our world as we allow desire in all its ways of being and knowing to heal us and make us whole at last.

Postscript: Desire, Mystery, Belonging and the Year of Covid-19

Today is March 11, 2021. This day, one year ago, was the day of the emergency announcement that the coronavirus was officially a global pandemic. That was the first day of what would become an unimaginable year.

Today feels like a holy day. I am deeply aware of my gratitude for still being alive and my horror at how many were not so fortunate. My mind struggles to comprehend how much has been lost. We are swimming in a grief that is collective and individual all at once. We are not the same and never will be again. We are new now, and we will learn who we are now in the days and years to come.

On March 11, 2020, I was packing to fly to Richmond, Virginia on March 12th. This would be the final of five sessions of Amber Karnes' inaugural Body Positive Yoga Teacher Training, a session that would last eight days. I had started the training program in October 2019 along with fourteen other students. I had been increasingly drawn to studying with Amber after meeting her at a women's retreat on Cape Cod in 2018. I had first tried yoga in 2002 and practiced it intermittently over the years, but as time went on, I felt compelled to learn more. I wanted to learn the whole of yoga—the philosophy and spirituality. I wanted to learn how to make yoga accessible and welcoming for anyone, any body, any soul. Amber's students, our group, were learning to become ruckus-makers. I loved these friends, and I was excited to spend more time with them.

So I was packing for my eight-day trip with an apartment rental already paid for. I was so excited to go, but I was also scared of the coronavirus. No one seemed to know yet exactly how much of a problem this would become. That afternoon, I talked with my husband, who encouraged me to go to Richmond. I called Amber and said that I was coming, but that I needed her to know that I was scared on a deep level. I thought perhaps this might be just the anxiety that often showed up for me in times of uncertainty, but something inside pushed me to reach out to Amber. I felt better after talking with her and decided to just go ahead and fly to Richmond the next day. Amber said that things would be as safe as she could make them.

Later that same evening, Amber texted me and said she was notifying all the students that she had decided to cancel our in-person training and shift to online teaching. She said that she had reached out to other yoga teacher trainers across the country, and even as the pandemic was being declared a global emergency, she made the decision to pivot to virtual learning for our final eight days of training.

One of our first teachers in Amber's training was Michelle Cassandra Johnson. She taught us so much, but the words she engraved on my heart were, "Expect and accept non-closure." These words were developed in collaboration with Dismantling Racism Works, a collective that Michelle was a part of, as one of a set of agreements for students. How could it be that these very words would become a life and death watchword over the next year? How could it be that after years in a career of seeking closure as a professional goal, I and we would live into a year of pure non-closure? How could it be that we would come to both expect and do our best to accept this non-closure?

It felt like this was the beginning of the end. We went through eight days in a row together on Zoom for most of each day with a break for lunch. By the time we had finished, we were close to graduating from our 200-hour training, only needing to complete our individual projects. We were new yoga teachers in a new world, and there was so much to absorb and live into.

I wrote earlier about the deaths of my father and mother. Not even three weeks after finishing our yoga teacher training, one of my sisters died unexpectedly in her sleep. As the pandemic closed in on us, the paramedics would not let me enter her house. The medical examiner decided there was no need for an autopsy as she had a history of heart disease. My other sisters could not travel to be with us for another two months, when we were finally able to have a small, private memorial service with a maximum of ten of her family and close friends present. The service helped, but because of Covid, it could not be the service we would have wanted. Accepting the painful and sudden loss of our sister brought so much sadness. The traditional rituals of death and grief were upended over and over again. I missed my sister deep in my aching heart, and loss prevailed everywhere else in our world as well.

There was so much more trauma. There was political upheaval and division like I had never known. Injustice in the streets and systemic racism were made even worse by the pandemic complications. In time, a weeklong winter storm that plunged my own state of Texas into a deep freeze would be followed by power outages and loss of water. And (as of the final edits for this book) over 800,000 souls in our United States would die from Covid-19. Loss that will take beyond the rest of my life to comprehend. Loss that can never be reconciled.

We all know this story now. We know the glimmering light of the vaccine. I am so grateful for my own two doses. I lay awake in bed, shivering with chills after my second dose, thanking God at 3:00 am for the hope of safety at last. Knowing still that hope too means expecting and accepting non-closure.

So, what about desire, mystery, and belonging? As I, as all of us, have surrendered many things this past year, what about these words, these themes, these ways of being? The book I wrote is about desire, mystery, and belonging, and most of it was retrospective. I wrote about what I have come to know as a spiritual path for myself and many others. So how about this past year? What can I say today about desire, mystery, and belonging now that we are almost two years into this pandemic and into all the other disruption and heartbreak and trauma that has emerged alongside the coronavirus? Does it hold true even now? Though days are passing and progress is being made, it does not erase our loss. What can desire, mystery, and belonging offer us as we look to an uncertain future?

Paraphrasing St. Bonaventure again: "If you want to know God, follow your deepest desire." Many times during this past year, our deepest desire has been to survive: to survive Covid-19, to escape infection, to have our memories be a blessing. Desire in its deepest geography keeps us seeking, keeps us alive. It is imagination and it is hope.

Be the "most you" that you can be. We become our truest selves when we are up against a wall. The wall of desperation in the face of devastating illness, of fear, of injustice that screams of unspeakable loss. Here we can fall into our true selves and seek our deepest desire that may have never dared to speak its name. Here we can touch the face of the Holy.

Mystery is familiar to us now. So much more familiar than we might have ever known. Mystery, uncertainty, the unknown all became the river at flood stage, the hurricane approaching our shore, the lightning that struck seemingly at random. Mystery became for us a literal force of nature. I found myself clinging to Michelle Cassandra Johnson's words over and over, day in and day out. The words "expect and accept non-closure" felt like medicine for my soul. They did not change what was happening, but they guided my soul all the way through. Life is like this sometimes. I now understand that mystery is inescapable if we keep our eyes and minds and spirits open. And that mystery is how time moves forward. It is by mystery that we can know that we are alive and changing and growing through cycles and seasons. Mystery keeps us moving. It is curiosity and it is hope.

If desire is the flame within that enlivens and animates us, and if mystery is the raging river and the unexpected phone call that leaves us breathless or in tears, then belonging is the neighbor, the bridge, the knitting needles that bring and keep us together. Together with ourselves, together with each other, together with the Holy, belonging is how our desire comes into the world around us, and belonging is how we survive the mystery. The power of belonging is that it can be ever-changing and simultaneously faithful across generations. Belonging is common humanity, and if there ever was a time in my life when I knew this deeply and profoundly, it has been these Covid-19 times. Belonging is necessary for life, and it is hope.

Rumi teaches us, "There are a thousand ways to kneel and kiss the ground." There are an infinite number of ways to travel through our lives on our spiritual journey. Honoring the past, opening to the future, and accepting both requires that we be present to the now. Present to the present. It is in the present that desire, mystery, and belonging can be our companions, our bookmarks, our touchstones. It is in the future that we will live into the desire, mystery, and belonging that we choose, that awaits us, that will always find us. This is one of many paths, and perhaps this is woven into all paths.

We learn as we go. Life is like this. Love is like this, too. My prayer is that this book has offered you bread for the journey and hope for the days to come. I also pray that our paths may cross again in the future.

May we honor our desire deep within again and again, and may we always warm our hearts at our own internal fire of desire. May we learn to find love in the mystery as we carry our own light and desire through times that are uncertain and challenging. May we trust in belonging in all its many faces and allow ourselves, others, and the Holy to love and uphold us on every journey. I pray that we will recognize and know the light that is within us, around us, and beyond us. I hold you and all of us in my heart.

ACKNOWLEDGMENTS

I am grateful to so many.

Martina Faulkner, president, and founder of IOM, said yes to this book and yes to me. You held the door open and invited me to come in. You and IOM are my miracle.

Winter Murray supported this book and me in so many ways. You are supportive, responsive, respectful, and wise, and I learned to trust the editing and publishing processes from you and your work.

Jennifer Louden, author and my longtime teacher, coach, and friend, created and held space for my writing and for me, always took me seriously, and saw me as a writer long before I saw myself as one. You were my beloved book birthing doula, you gave me so many dear friends, and you taught me to have faith that being myself is always the best choice.

W. Andrew Achenbaum, professor and friend, is the honorary godfather of this book. You helped me believe in this book and in my own writing, and you are an extraordinary chief encourager and connector.

Barbara Lewis was my spiritual director for seventeen years. You brought me into the shared presence of the Holy repeatedly, through life events and changes, and you helped me to see and hear and feel and know the love and wholeness that always waits in this sacred Presence. I am so grateful for your friendship and love.

All who are in this book are in my own heart for all my days. You generously allowed me to share the crossings of our paths and the telling of our stories together.

Desire, Mystery, and Belonging

Trinity Episcopal Church in Midtown Houston has been the community of my spirit for years now. You welcomed me and shared joy and sadness and sacraments and laughter with me, and I learned about belonging in a new and powerful way from all of you.

All my friends, all my writing companions, and all my beta readers have deeply touched my life. You are all the absolute best company on this amazing journey.

All my family, my parents, grandparents, sisters, aunts, uncles, cousins, nieces, nephews, and the ones we married and their families, have loved each other and have loved me. You are all signs of grace to me, and I am the luckiest soul to be part of our greater belonging across generations.

Bob and Katie are my whole heart and soul. Our life together has been, is, and will always be everything to me.

I send all my gratitude and abundant love to each of you, to all of you.

ABOUT THE AUTHOR

Sarah Robinson Flick has been a listener for over thirty years. In 2016, she left her longtime position as a psychiatrist medical director in a large public mental health center to focus on a "third act" that includes writing, offering spiritual direction to clergy and others, and traveling. Sarah has long believed in the calling of vocation and seeks to follow paths that support healing and wholeness. She is inspired by the season of autumn, great movies, visits to sacred places, the courage of those who work for social justice, and the presence of the Holy in everyday life. Sarah especially loves reading books of all kinds and gelato, as well as spending time with her daughter Katie and husband Bob, an Episcopal priest, with whom she lives in Texas. *Desire, Mystery, and Belonging* is her first book.

Printed in Great Britain
by Amazon

30807617R00128